Best Recipes of Illinois Inns and Restaurants

Edited and Compiled by:
Margaret E. Guthrie

Editorial Assistance:
Annie L.J. Saart

First edition.

Library of Congress Catalog Number: 88-71881

ISBN: 0-942495-04-7

Others in this series:
Best Recipes of Michigan Inns and Restaurants
Best Recipes of Minnesota Inns and Restaurants
Best Recipes of Ohio Inns and Restaurants
Best Recipes of Wisconsin Inns and Restaurants

For additional copies of this book, or others in the series, contact:

Amherst Press
A division of Palmer Publications, Inc.
P.O. Box 296
Amherst, Wisconsin 54406

Table of Contents

Preface

On this, our fifth book, the team that turns these books out is in place and well practiced—my publisher Chuck Spanbauer and his talented and dedicated staff, my assistant Annie Saart, who copy edits, and my three children who maintain my sense of humor.

On this book, the list of local "spies" is too long to enumerate, but you know who you are and you have our thanks.

Introduction

The first thing you discover when doing a book like this about Illinois is that there is good food, and lots of it, outside Chicago. We deliberately chose not to include Chicago in this book, feeling that it is too large for our scope and it is better, when dealing with food particularly, not to attempt something than to do it badly.

Also, Chicago has been done a number of times. There are at least four guidebooks to dining in Chicago and while they may not contain recipes, they do tell you where to eat, catering to your every possible gustatory whim.

This book then, is a guide to suburban Chicago and other parts of Illinois and some of the food available as you travel around the state. I think you will agree that there are some interesting prospects in store.

Unfortunately, with this book I must report an important failure. In Springfield, Illinois' capital, there is a dish called a horseshoe. It consists of two slices of good bread on which you put several slices of ham. This is topped with a special cheese sauce, which is then topped with french fried potatoes.

No one was willing to part with their special cheese sauce recipe, but I venture to guess that if you have a good hand with a Welsh rarebit or cheese fondue, you can duplicate the horseshoe. The name, I am told, derives from the cut of ham first used in this creation—the horseshoe cut. For those of faint appetite, a ponyshoe, consisting of one slice of bread, has been ordained as acceptable.

Illinois is the fifth in this series and, as with the others in the series, I have discovered that there is good food available everywhere—it is simply a matter of locating it. It is heartening to find that we are not completely at the mercy of the fast food chains as we travel, that we can set out and expect and obtain reasonable and even delicious food on the road.

Illinois is a state with much to offer, in particular a lot of history which is interesting to trace. From Illinois chefs and cooks here's food to try along the way and then come home and cook yourself. Bon appetit.

****

Before you set out to recreate these recipes, there are some things Illinois' chefs, like chefs everywhere, ask you to consider. First, read each recipe you intend to prepare all the way through before beginning to cook. Be sure that you have all the ingredients on hand before you begin and do not substitute one ingredient for another. For instance, do not substitute yellow salad mustard for Dijon-style mustard. One chef reported an angry customer who claimed he had left out a "secret ingredient" and that's why she was unable to duplicate his creation. Patiently he led her through the recipe to discover that she had substituted canned spinach for fresh!

About the ingredients: flour means all purpose white flour. If another flour is called for it will be specified, as in unbleached or whole wheat. Eggs are large unless specified. Butter means butter—unsalted, clarified or whipped will be specified. Sugar is the same, being white granulated unless otherwise indicated. Most of the recipes call for heavy cream, which is slightly heavier than whipping and less likely to be "ultra-pasteurized." Ultra-pasteurization makes the cream flat and tasteless but gives it a long shelf life. Who, for heaven's sake, wants cream that has a long shelf life? Ask your grocer for regular heavy cream, not ultra-pasteurized. If enough of us protest, we can have our good cream back again. The good stuff is frequently labeled heavy "gourmet" cream.

Use the freshest ingredients—you will be surprised at the difference it makes, and it really does not take a lot longer to squeeze a little lemon juice than to open a bottle. And please, please grate the parmesan and romano cheeses. You will be astounded at the sharpness and liveliness of the taste. Squeeze the lemon and grate the cheese. There is no comparison when it comes to taste and to flavor.

Brunch

Brunch

Brunch is a pleasant custom which seems to have come into its own with the multiplication of women in the work force. It's an easy way to entertain, whether you take your guests out to your favorite restaurant or do it at home.

Almost any dish is a legitimate brunch dish as long as it is relatively easy to prepare, can expand to feed more than orginally planned and tempt the guests to leave bare plates and request the recipe.

Here are some examples of what Illinois eats for brunch.

Cajun Andouille Cream Sauce
with Tortellini

3 tablespoons butter
3 tablespoons flour
½ cup diced Spanish onion
½ cup diced bell pepper
½ cup diced celery
1 pound smoked Andouille
  sausage, sliced*
1 garlic clove, crushed
1 teaspoon cayenne pepper
1 teaspoon black pepper
1 teaspoon paprika
½ teaspoon salt
1 quart heavy cream

*Andouille is a special Cajun sausage, available at specialty butchers or by mail order: K-Paul's Louisiana Mail Order Catalogue, 500 Mandeville Street, P. O. Box 770034, New Orleans, LA 70177-0034.

In a cast iron skillet, melt the butter and mix in the flour. Continue to whisk until mixture becomes nut-brown in color. Don't worry about the mixture burning as long as you are whisking; don't leave the roux unattended, however.

Add the onion, pepper and celery, stirring constantly. Cook for 1-2 minutes. Add the sausage and seasonings and stir for 1 more minute. Slowly add the heavy cream, continuing to stir as you do so. Continue stirring until hot and thick, about 4-6 minutes.

Cook the tortellini according to directions and ladle the hot cream sauce over the tortellini. Serve with a good crusty bread and a dry red wine. Yield: 4 servings.

From: **The North End Market Restaurant**
395 North Kinzie Street
Bradley

The Frittata

9 eggs
1½ cups freshly grated
   parmesan cheese
1 tablespoon granulated garlic
1 teaspoon crushed red pepper
2 cups sautéed spinach
olive oil for sautéing
1 cup grated mozzarella
   cheese
1 cup diced cooked potatoes

Whip the eggs until frothy. Blend in the parmesan cheese, garlic and red pepper. Drain the chopped spinach well and fold into the mixture.

Preheat the oven to 450 degrees. Heat a large (12-inch) skillet well. Add a little olive oil and turn to coat the pan. Pour in the batter all at once, stir as you would for an omelet.

When the mixture begins to set, drop in the diced potatoes evenly, then sprinkle with the mozzarella.

Place the entire pan in the oven till set and the mozzarella begins to brown.

When done, carefully slide the frittata onto a warm serving platter and cut into wedges as you would a pie. A dry white wine is best with this dish. Yield: 6 servings.

From: **The North End
         Market Restaurant**
         395 North Kinzie Street
         Bradley

Goulash

2½ pounds good stew beef,
   cubed, ¾-inch
1½ large onions, diced
1 tablespoon margarine
2½ tablespoons paprika

Cut the meat into cubes, discarding any fat and gristle. Cook the onions in the margarine until shiny, then add the paprika. Stir to combine, cook for 3 minutes and then add the Burgundy.

⅓ cup Burgundy
1 cup water with bouillon cube or
* 1 cup good beef stock*
¼ cup tomato paste
¼ teaspoon pepper
¼ teaspoon garlic salt
1 bay leaf
3 tablespoons Worcestershire
* sauce*
4 cups fresh mushrooms, sliced
½ large or 1 medium potato,
* grated*

Add the meat and cook until all the redness is gone and the pan is full of juices. Add the water/stock, tomato paste, pepper, garlic salt, bay leaf, Worcestershire, and mushrooms. Bring to a simmer and cook for half an hour or until meat is tender. Add the potato and cook for another 15 minutes.

From: **Eberhard's**
           117 North Main Street
           Columbia

Hobo Hash

This is a signature dish of the Farmers' Home Hotel in Galena. This recipe is for one serving. For a crowd, simply multiply by the number of guests.

melted butter or oil
1 russet (baking) potato
* parboiled, diced ½-inch*
2 ounces chopped onion
2 ounces chopped fresh broccoli
2-3 ounces cooked, chopped
* bacon, ham or Canadian bacon*
salt and pepper to taste
2-3 ounces shredded
* cheddar cheese*

In a heavy skillet, put the butter or oil. Add the potato, onion, broccoli and the bacon or ham. "Stir fry" quickly and then put a lid on the pan to steam the broccoli al dente. Sprinkle with salt and pepper to taste and top with the cheese. Allow it to melt and then add a dollop of sour cream if desired. Serve with eggs and toast. Yield: 1 serving.

From: **The Farmers'**
           Home Hotel
           334 Spring Street
           Galena

Macaroni and Cheese Pudding

4 cups macaroni
8 tablespoons unsalted butter
¾ cup flour
4 cups boiling milk
1 cup grated Swiss cheese
2 cups grated cheddar cheese
½ cup chopped sweet pepper
salt and pepper to taste

Cook the macaroni until al dente, drain and set aside. Melt the butter in a heavy bottomed saucepan and add the flour, whisking continuously. Cook over low heat 3-5 minutes until the roux is lightly browned.

Gradually add the hot milk to the roux, continuing to stir until thoroughly blended. Then add in the cheeses, continuing to stir to blend evenly and smoothly. When cheeses have melted, add in the sweet pepper and season to taste.

Mix the cheese with the macaroni and serve immediately or place in a buttered pan and reheat in the oven at 350 degrees. Yield: 6 entrée size portions or 12 side dishes.

From: **The Public Landing Restaurant**
200 West 8th Street
Lockport

Sausage Spinach Quiche

Pie crust:
1 cup flour
pinch of salt
6 tablespoons butter
5 tablespoons cold milk

Filling:
4 eggs
1 cup heavy cream
½ pound fresh spinach
½ pound sausage
salt and pepper to taste

Preheat oven to 450 degrees. For the pie crust, sift flour and salt into a bowl, cut in the butter. Add the cold milk and mix until mixture forms a ball and pulls away from the sides of the bowl. Roll the dough out on a floured surface with a floured rolling pin. Line a 9-inch pan and prick with a fork, being careful not to prick all the way through. You want the pie crust not to puff up in pre-cooking, but you don't want the filling to leak through later.

Bake in the oven 6-8 minutes. Remove and cool.

Preheat oven to 375 degrees. Blend eggs and cream in a bowl. Clean and cook the spinach just until wilted. Drain and set aside. Cook and crumble the sausage. Drain and set aside. Add the spinach and sausage to the egg mixture. Salt and pepper to taste. Pour mixture into the prebaked pie shell. Bake in oven for 30-35 minutes until browned and puffy on top.

From:

Chez Seamus
French Cafe
The Village at Ginger Creek, #10
Edwardsville

Spinach Pie or Spanakopita

5 10-ounce packages frozen
   spinach, cooked and drained
1 pound feta cheese, crumbled
1 pound large curd
   cottage cheese
2 medium onions, grated
olive oil
6 eggs
1 bunch green onions
1 bunch parsley, chopped
fresh dill weed
1 package phyllo dough
½ cup melted butter
½ teaspoon black pepper

Cook the spinach according to package directions and wring out, being sure the spinach is quite dry. Place in a large mixing bowl. Add the feta cheese, well crumbled, then the cottage cheese. Fry the onions in a little olive oil until brown and add these to the spinach cheese mixture.

Beat the eggs slightly and add to the spinach cheese mixture. Add the chopped green onions and parsley and fresh dill weed, if available, to taste.

Preheat oven to 350 degrees. Take the package of phyllo dough, which you have defrosted carefully and unwrap. Place 6 layers of phyllo in a baking pan, buttering each layer with the melted butter.

Place the spinach filling on the six layers and top with the remaining six layers, buttering each as you lay it on top.

Bake for 20-30 minutes until golden brown. Yield: 8-10 servings.

From: **Nick's Cafe**
480 Brush College Road
Decatur

Smoked Trout Cheesecake

Crust:
2 cups roasted, finely
   chopped hazelnuts
6 tablespoons butter

Filling:
24 ounces cream cheese, cubed
6 eggs
1 pint sour cream
1/3 cup sifted flour
grated zest of 1 lemon
grated zest of 1/2 lime
grated zest of 1/2 orange
juice of 1/2 lemon
1 1/2 cup flaked smoked trout
1 cup chopped green onions
salt and pepper to taste
Tabasco sauce to taste

Mix 1½ cups of the nuts with the butter and use this to line the bottom of a 10-inch springform pan. Butter the sides of the pan well.

Preheat the oven to 350 degrees. Beat the cubed cream cheese until soft and creamy. Blend in the eggs one at a time until well blended. Add the sour cream, flour and the zests of lemon, lime and orange and the lemon juice. Mix well. Stir the smoked trout and green onions into the cheese mixture and add the salt, pepper and Tabasco to taste.

Pour the cheese mixture into the prepared pan and bake for one hour. Turn off the heat and allow the cheesecake to remain in the oven for another hour. Cool to room temperature. Sprinkle the remaining nuts on top of the cake. Chill overnight. Serve with Sweet and Sour Red Onions, whole grain mustard, diced tomatoes and cornichons.

From: **Maldaner's**
222 South Sixth Street
Springfield

Sweet and Sour Red Onions

1 cup red wine vinegar
1 cup sugar
2 red onions, sliced thin
2 tablespoons capers with juice

Bring red wine vinegar to a boil in a non-reactive saucepan. Add the sugar and reduce by one quarter. Pour over the onions, then add the capers and let stand at room temperature, stirring occasionally. Serve with Smoked Trout Cheesecake.

From: **Maldaner's**
                    222 South Sixth Street
                             Springfield

Bread & Rolls

Bread & Rolls

Bread is one of those foods too much taken for granted. In this country, after succumbing for a time to pasty, white unhealthy bread wrapped in plastic, we are again discovering the joys of eating good bread. Bread with crust, bread with body and most important of all, bread with taste. Bread that has some nourishment to it and is not just filler.

Here are a few breads from Illinois restaurants where bread is baked and served to those lucky enough to be patrons or to have found the place. Try some and see if you don't agree, real bread is worth the effort. It's easy to bake and not all that much trouble! Good eating.

Corn Sage Bread

1 tablespoon dry yeast or
   1 cake compressed
⅓ cup sugar, divided
¼ cup warm water
⅓ cup shortening
½ teaspoon sage
¼ cup onion flakes
1 tablespoon salt
1 cup evaporated milk and
   1 cup water or
   2 cups milk, scalded
3 cups unbleached flour
2 eggs, well beaten
1 cup yellow corn meal
4-4½ cups flour, divided

Preheat the oven to 375 degrees. Dissolve the yeast and 1 teaspoon of the sugar in the warm water in a small bowl. Let stand for 5-10 minutes or until mixture expands and becomes bubbly. Set aside.

Combine the shortening, remaining sugar, sage, onion and salt with the milk and water (or milk) in a large bowl. Stir until shortening melts.

Stir in unbleached flour. Add the eggs, the cornmeal and the reserved yeast mixture. Stir in 3½ cups of the flour. Gradually stir in enough of the remaining flour to make a stiff dough. Turn out on lightly-floured board. Knead for 10 minutes or until the dough is smooth and elastic. Dust board and dough with more flour if necessary to prevent sticking. Shape the dough into a ball. Place in a large, well greased bowl. Turn the dough to grease the top. Cover with a clean towel and let rise in a warm, draft-free place for 1-1½ hours, or until doubled in bulk. Punch down dough. Turn out on lightly-floured board. Cover and let rest for 10 minutes. Knead for 1-2 minutes. Cut in ½ and shape into 2 loaves. Grease 9 x 5 x 3-inch loaf pans. Place dough in pans. Cover and let rise in warm, draft-free place for 20 minutes, or until dough has risen to the rim of pans. Bake for 35-45 minutes or until crust is brown and the top sounds hollow when rapped with a knuckle. Remove from pans, cool on a rack. Yield: 2 loaves.

From: **Elsah's Landing
Restaurant**
18 LaSalle Street
Elsah

Corn Bread

¼ cup sugar
6 eggs
4⅛ cups milk
1⅛ cups flour
2½ cups stone ground corn meal
2½ tablespoons baking powder
1 teaspoon salt
¼ cup bacon fat, melted

Preheat the oven to 425 degrees. Grease a 9 x 12-inch pan. Combine the sugar, eggs, milk, beat well.

Sift together the flour, corn meal, baking powder and salt and add to the liquid mixture. Fold in the melted bacon fat.

Bake for 15-20 minutes or until done. The cornbread should be a golden brown around the edges. Serve immediately.

From: **Central Station Cafe**
220 East Front Street
Bloomington

Egg Bread

2 cups warm water
¼ cup sugar
¼ cup butter, softened
2 teaspoons salt
3 eggs
2 tablespoons yeast
7 + cups unbleached flour

Mix together the warm water (about 110 degrees) and the sugar. Add in the butter, salt, eggs and yeast, mix well. Gradually add in the flour until a stiff dough has formed.

Either knead the bread dough in a machine, if you have one, or turn it out on a lightly-floured board. Knead the bread dough until it

becomes smooth and elastic. Place in a well-greased or buttered bowl and turn and allow to rise in a warm, draft-free place for an hour or so, or until the dough has doubled in bulk.

Punch down and knead again for a few minutes. The dough is then ready to make the following:

For Braided Bread: Preheat oven to 350 degrees. Divide the dough in half. Take each half and divide in thirds. Roll out each third with your hands until you have an even roll about 18 inches long. Braid these and tuck the ends under. Place on a baking sheet sprinkled with cornmeal. Cover and allow to rise again for about 20 minutes or half an hour. If desired, loaves may be washed with an egg wash made with an egg beaten with a little cold water and then sprinkled with the seeds of your choice—sesame, poppy or caraway. Bake 45 minutes to an hour or until done. Crust should be a golden brown and loaf should sound hollow when rapped with a knuckle.

To make Dinner Rolls: Preheat oven to 375 degrees. Grease a 12-cup muffin tin. Break off small pieces of dough, roll them smooth between your hands and place in the greased muffin cups. Cover and let rise again for a few minutes, till the rolls are at the level of the pan. Again, you may wash with an egg wash and sprinkle with your favorite seeds. Bake until done, about 10-15 minutes.

For Onion Sandwich Rolls: Preheat oven to 375 degrees. Cut about 1-ounce pieces, larger if you want larger rolls. Mix together chopped onions, poppy seeds and a little oil. Dip rounded pieces of dough into the onion mixture. Place on baking sheet on which you have sprinkled corn meal. Flatten slightly. Press on more of the onion mixture if desired. Allow to rise slightly and bake until the tops are golden brown. These make terrific sandwich rolls.

From: **The Intermezzo Cafe**
Krannert Center
for the Performing Arts
Urbana

Raised Garlic Balls

½ cup + 2 tablespoons milk
2 tablespoons butter
pinch of salt
1 tablespoon dry yeast
2-2¼ cups flour
1 egg
1½ tablespoons garlic powder
1 tablespoon sugar
oil for deep frying
garlic salt

Generously oil a large bowl and set aside. Pour milk into a small saucepan and heat until scalded. Transfer to a mixing bowl and add butter and salt. Cool to lukewarm. Add yeast and let stand 5 minutes. Mix in 1 cup flour, beating with wooden spoon until smooth. Blend in egg, garlic powder, and sugar. Beat in remaining flour and knead by hand on lightly floured surface until smooth and elastic, or mix in flour with heavy duty electric mixer fitted with dough hook, beating until dough pulls away from the side of the bowl, about 3-5 minutes. Transfer to the oiled bowl, cover with a clean, damp towel and let stand in warm place until doubled in bulk or about 45 minutes. Turn out on lightly-floured surface. Roll or pat to ½-inch thickness. Use a small round cutter, about 1 inch in diameter, (the center of doughnut cutter works well) to shape dough. Place on lightly-floured baking sheet and let stand for 15 minutes. Heat the oil to 350 degrees. Deep fry the garlic balls several at a time until golden brown. Drain on paper towels. Sprinkle with garlic salt and serve at once.

From: **The Westerfield House**
Rural Route 2
Freeburg

Westerfield House Cream Fingers

These would be wonderful with afternoon tea!

slightly stale,
  good sandwich bread
softened cream cheese
melted butter
cinnamon and sugar,
  mixed together or
  good homemade jam
finely ground nuts

Preheat oven to 350 degrees. Cut the crusts from the bread and roll flat with a rolling pin. Spread with the cream cheese. Roll up like a jelly roll. Roll in the melted butter and then in the cinnamon-sugar mixture.

Or spread with the cream cheese, then with your favorite jam and roll up. Roll in the melted butter, then in the ground nuts. Place on baking sheet and bake 15-20 minutes. These are best served shortly after baking, serve warm or at room temperature.

From: **The Westerfield House**
Rural Route 2
Freeburg

BREAD & ROLLS

Appetizers

Appetizers

Whether you call them hors d'oeuvres, antipasti, tapas or appetizers, they serve the same purpose and taste as good. Designed to whet the appetite, as a forecast of even better things to come, they are wonderful palate teasers and pleasers.

Often an appetizer is good enough to stand alone with good bread and a bottle of your favorite wine. Try some of these from Illinois and see if you don't agree.

Baked Brie

6 frozen pastry shells or
make your own

Sauce:
1 8-ounce package frozen
raspberries
4 ounces good quality
raspberry preserves
2 ounces port wine
6 ounces brie, cubed,
cut from small wheels
fresh raspberries, honeydew
melon, kiwi, or appropriate
seasonal fruit as garnish

Bake the pastry shells according to package directions or make your own.

Combine the frozen raspberries, the raspberry jam and the port wine in a heavy bottomed non-reactive saucepan. Simmer over low heat for 15 minutes. Strain.

Place the cubed brie in the center of each pastry shell. Preheat oven to 400 degrees. Just before serving time, place the pastry shells with brie in the oven for about 5 minutes or just until the brie begins to warm and soften.

Place sauce on 6 serving plates, put a pastry shell with warmed brie on each plate and garnish with the fresh fruit, which also serves as an accompaniment. Yield: 6 servings.

From: **Eagle Ridge Inn
& Resort**
Highway 20 East
Galena

Fried Catfish Nuggets
with Homemade Tartar Sauce

Catfish:
2-3 pounds fresh catfish filets
2 cups flour
1 cup cornmeal
½ teaspoon cayenne pepper
1 teaspoon white pepper
1 teaspoon salt
6 eggs
flour

Tartar Sauce:
2 whole eggs
2 egg yolks
2 tablespoons lemon juice
¼ cup vinegar
2 tablespoons salt
2 cups peanut oil
½ cup chopped onions
¼ cup chopped parsley
⅛ cup fresh lemon juice
¼ cup sweet relish

Cut the catfish into bite-size pieces. Mix together the flour, cornmeal and seasonings. Beat the eggs thoroughly.

Dip the catfish nuggets into the flour, then into the eggs, and finally into the cornmeal-flour mixture. Fry at 375 to 400 degrees until golden.

In the food processor or blender, blend the eggs, the yolks, lemon juice, vinegar, and salt. While machine is running, slowly add the oil so it is blended thoroughly.

Fold in the onions, parsley, lemon juice and sweet relish.

From: **The Public Landing**
200 West 8th Street
Lockport

Macadamia Dip

8 ounces cream cheese,
  softened
2 tablespoons milk
2½ ounces chipped beef
⅓ cup finely chopped
  green pepper
½ teaspoon garlic salt
¼ teaspoon pepper
1 teaspoon onion flakes
2-3 teaspoons horseradish
½ cup sour cream
½ cup coarsely chopped
  macadamia nuts
2 teaspoons butter

Preheat oven to 350 degrees. Combine the cream cheese and the milk. Add the chipped beef, bell pepper, garlic salt, pepper, onion flakes and horseradish. Fold in sour cream. Spoon into shallow baking dish. In a small frying pan, glaze the macadamia nuts in butter. Sprinkle nuts over the cream cheese mixture. Bake for 20 minutes. Serve hot with crackers. Yield: 12 servings.

From: **The Westerfield House**
Rural Route 2
Freeburg

Oysters Autumn Tree

30 fresh Gulf oysters
4 ounces chablis
2 medium red onions, diced
2 ounces clarified butter
1½ teaspoons dill weed
8 ounces freshly grated
    parmesan cheese
salt and pepper to taste
¾ teaspoon thyme
4 ounces Burgundy
4 ounces brandy
8 ounces white sauce*
16 ounces bearnaise sauce
fresh parsley
paprika

*White Sauce:
1 ounce chablis
2 ounces fresh chicken stock
½ teaspoon ham base
8 ounces milk
4 ounces heavy cream
½ bay leaf
1 teaspoon salt
½ teaspoon freshly ground
    white pepper
3 ounces clarified butter
3 ounces flour

Bearnaise Sauce:
½ cup red wine vinegar
2 ounces Burgundy
1 medium red onion, diced
4 tablespoons tarragon
1 teaspoon onion powder
6 egg yolks
1½ teaspoons salt
⅛ teaspoon cayenne pepper

Preheat oven to 350 degrees. Place the freshly shucked oysters on a sheet pan and top with the chablis, half of the red onion, the dill weed, half the parmesan cheese. Bake until the cheese browns.

In a saucepan sauté the remaining half of the red onion until crispy along with the salt, pepper, and thyme. Add the Burgundy and brandy and flame. When alcohol has cooked out, add the white sauce and blend well. Remove the oysters from the oven and add the onion sauce and the other half of the parmesan cheese. Cook again until brown. When done, remove and top with bearnaise sauce. Sprinkle parsley and paprika over top and serve immediately. Yield: 6 servings.

For the white sauce, combine the wine, chicken stock, and ham base and reduce to ¾. Set aside. Heat the milk and cream with the bay leaf, salt and pepper to 180 degrees in a double boiler. While the milk is heating, heat butter to the smoking point and add the flour and stir over medium heat for 2 minutes to make a pale roux. Set aside. When milk is heated to 180 degrees, heat roux, if necessary, and add the milk in four equal amounts, stirring well each time. Add the reduced wine stock and simmer for an hour stirring occasionally. Thin with more chicken stock if desired.

For the bearnaise sauce, combine the red wine vinegar, Burgundy, onion, tarragon and onion powder, reducing to 1 tablespoon. Set aside. Combine egg yolks, salt, cayenne pepper, chablis, Worcestershire sauce, brandy and Tabasco. Over a double boiler cook until it begins to thicken. The whisk should leave lines in the mixture. Add the water and mix. Add butter slowly in a steady stream, whisk-

1 ounce chablis
½ ounce Worcestershire sauce
4 ounces brandy
12 drops Tabasco
1 tablespoon water

ing constantly until all the butter is incorporated. Add the reduced red wine mixture and blend well. Serve.

From: **The Autumn Tree**
307 South Prairie Street
Champaign

Pecan Breaded Oysters
with Fresh Vanilla,
Cucumbers and Tomatoes

16 oysters, on the half shell
5 ounces pecans
8 ounces flour
2 vanilla beans, split
1 cucumber, peeled, seeded
3-4 plum tomatoes,
  peeled, seeded, diced
4 ounces heavy cream
4 ounces unsalted butter
fresh herbs and Italian parsley
  for garnish

Shuck oysters, reserve the bottom shells. Grind the pecans in the food processor or blender. Add the flour.

Dust the oysters with the pecan flour mixture. Sauté in a non-stick pan with a little butter or vegetable oil. Reserve and keep warm.

Combine the vanilla, cucumbers, tomatoes and cream and bring to a boil. Reduce slightly, allowing the flavor of the vanilla to come out. Add the butter, bit by bit, stirring after each addition, until all the butter has been blended into the sauce.

Place four oyster shells on each serving plate. Pour some sauce in each shell. Put the remaining sauce on the plates. Put oysters in each shell, cut the vanilla beans into quarter-inch lengths, use on plates for contrast of color. Garnish with fresh herbs and Italian parsley. Yield: 4 servings.

From: **Melange Restaurant**
1515 Sheridan, Plaza del Lago
Wilmette

Pâté

2½ ounces dry sherry
1 ounce brandy
1 ounce cognac
1 pound, 4 ounces butter
1 pound chicken livers
1 medium red onion, julienne
1 teaspoon freshly ground
   black pepper
½ teaspoon garlic powder
½ teaspoon basil
½ teaspoon thyme
⅜ teaspoon curry powder
⅜ teaspoon dill weed
¼ teaspoon onion powder
¼ teaspoon filé powder
¼ teaspoon poultry seasoning
½ tablespoon Worcestershire
   sauce
3 drops Tabasco
dash white pepper
dash cayenne pepper
1-1½ teaspoons salt
fresh parsley
paprika

Combine sherry, brandy and cognac. Reduce to 1 ounce taking care not to burn by shaking sauté pan constantly over the burner. Set aside.

Divide the butter in half and put one half in the freezer. Put the other half in a medium saucepan. Remove all fat from the chicken livers and place in the pan. Add the onion and all spices except salt, which will toughen the livers as they cook. Over medium heat cook the chicken livers until pink. Livers must be constantly stirred to avoid breaking the sauce. If sauce does break, remove pan from heat and continue stirring until livers are done. After cooking the livers, add the reduced liquors. Remove the other half of the butter from the freezer and divide into 6 pieces. Incorporate one at a time into the sauce. Even if the sauce broke, it will come together at this point, provided that the butter is well chilled. Last, add the salt and adjust the seasoning. Put the mixture in the blender or food processor and blend or process at high speed until well combined. Chill for 12 hours before serving. Serve with toast points, red onion rings and sliced hard boiled eggs with parsley and paprika sprinkled over the top. Yield: 6-8 servings.

From:　**The Autumn Tree**
307 South Prairie Street
Champaign

Porino Moruno

1½-2 pounds sirloin tip, cubed
green and red peppers,
    cut into strips
5 onions, cut into eighths

Marinade:
3 tablespoons olive oil
1 small onion, minced
2 cloves garlic, minced
1 tablespoon fresh parsley
1 teaspoon Spanish paprika
½ dried red chili pepper,
    seeded and crushed or
    ¼ teaspoon red pepper seeds
¼ teaspoon dried oregano or
    1 tablespoon fresh
⅛ teaspoon fresh cumin
salt to taste
freshly ground black pepper
1-2 cans tomato juice or
vegetable juice

Prepare marinade by blending together all ingredients in a shallow non-reactive or glass bowl.

Cube the sirloin tip into 1-inch cubes. Place four of each, sirloin, pepper and onion on a skewer and place in marinade.

Marinate for several days in the refrigerator. Then cook the pinchos on a hot grill, being sure to cook on all four sides, until done. This recipe produces a lot of smoke, so you must be careful of that. The pinchos can be cooked in the oven at 350 degrees to avoid the smoke. They can also be cooked outside on the grill, which would avoid the smoke problem. Serve with hot French bread slices.

If you are bold, the marinade may be used as a sauce. If kept refrigerated, the marinade may be used several times to make pinchos. Yield: 4-5 servings.

From: **The Kingston Inn**
         300 North Main Street
         Galena

Paillard of Fresh Salmon
with Horseradish Butter

2-3 pounds filet of fresh salmon

Horseradish Butter:
1 cup fish stock
2 tablespoons fresh lemon juice
1 tablespoon chopped shallots
½ teaspoon white pepper
¼ cup heavy cream
1 tablespoon fresh horseradish
4 ounces unsalted butter
salt to taste
⅛ cup capers

Preheat oven to 400 degrees. Remove the skin and bones of the salmon filets, cut into 1-inch steaks. Place 2 steaks between 2 sheets of plastic wrap and pound thin, to approximately ⅛ inch, with a rubber mallet.

Carefully transfer to an ovenproof plate.

Repeat to make 6 plates. Place in oven for about 2 minutes to cook medium rare. Serve with sauce immediately.

To make the sauce, reduce the fish stock, lemon juice, shallots and white pepper to 3-4 tablespoons over high heat.

Whisk in the cream, horseradish and butter. Finish the sauce with the salt and capers. Pour sauce down the middle of each plate and serve with toasted French bread. Yield: 6 servings.

From: **Tallgrass Restaurant**
1006 South State Street
Lockport

Smoked Salmon Mousse
with Garlic Croutons

4 ounces smoked salmon
8 ounces cream cheese
1 teaspoon fresh lemon juice
1 tablespoon sherry or brandy

Puree the salmon in the blender or food processor. Add the cream cheese, lemon juice and brandy or sherry. Puree and refrigerate.

baguettes*
butter
freshly grated parmesan
garlic pepper
grated red onion

*baguettes are long, thin loaves of
French bread

Preheat the oven to 350 degrees. Cut the baguettes in ½-inch slices, brush with butter, sprinkle with the parmesan and the garlic pepper. Bake on a cookie sheet in the oven until browned.

Pipe the salmon mousse mixture onto croutons and garnish with grated red onion. Or spoon a portion of salmon mousse mixture onto a lettuce leaf and serve with garlic croutons on side.

From: **Chez Seamus French Cafe**
The Village at Ginger Creek, #10
Edwardsville

Cassolettes de Scampi et Petoncles
Ramekins of Shrimps and Scallops

2 pounds spinach, trimmed
¾ pound scallops
1 pound medium shrimp, peeled
6 tablespoons clarified butter
salt and freshly ground pepper
2 cups peeled, seeded and
  chopped tomatoes
olive oil

Blanch the spinach in boiling salted water until barely tender. Drain well. Divide among individual shells or ramekins. Sauté scallops and shrimp in butter over medium high heat until the scallops turn opaque and the shrimp turn pink, about 4 minutes.

Remove from heat and season lightly with salt and pepper. Divide over spinach and top

Sauce Bearnaise:

½ cup red wine vinegar

3 tablespoons finely chopped
   shallots

1 tablespoon minced fresh
   tarragon or ½ teaspoon dried

2 teaspoons fresh minced
   chervil or ⅜ teaspoon dried

½ teaspoon salt

¼ teaspoon freshly
   ground pepper

4 egg yolks

8 ounces unsalted butter

¼ cup heavy cream

with bearnaise sauce. Run under a preheated broiler briefly until the top is golden, watching carefully to prevent scorching. Garnish with chopped tomato, lightly sautéed in the olive oil and serve immediately.

For the sauce, combine the first six ingredients in a heavy bottomed saucepan and bring to a boil over high heat. Reduce the heat and simmer until liquid is reduced to about 2 tablespoons, about 5 minutes. Let cool. Lightly whisk the egg yolks, add to the vinegar shallot mixture, blending well. Place the pan over low heat and whisk until mixture is thickened and becomes creamy, removing the pan from the heat occasionally as you whisk, to prevent yolks from curdling. Whisk in butter 1 piece at a time, blending completely before adding more. Continue whisking until sauce is the consistency of light mayonnaise. Cover and keep warm in bain marie. Just before serving, whip cream until stiff and fold into yolk mixture. Yield: 6-8 servings.

From: **Le Francais**
269 South Milwaukee
Wheeling

Soups

Soups

Soups are one my favorite foods to cook, to eat and to teach. I love them because they are nourishing to body and soul, and because they are generally forgiving so that the novice cook ends up with a dish that inspires pride and satisfies the appetite.

The chefs of Illinois did not let me down; here are recipes for soups as made in Illinois. The best soups, of course.

Asparagus Mushroom Soup

This rich cream soup has a marvelous fresh taste derived from its unusual combination.

4 cups chicken stock
½ pound fresh asparagus,
    washed, cut in ½-inch lengths
½ cup finely diced onion
6 tablespoons butter
3 tablespoons flour
½ pound fresh mushrooms,
    sliced
1 cup light cream
¼ teaspoon garlic salt
parsley

Bring the chicken stock to a simmer in a medium saucepan. Add the asparagus, cover and cook over medium heat for 10 minutes, or until asparagus is just tender.

Sauté the onion in the butter in medium saucepan over low heat for 10 minutes or until onion is golden brown. Blend in the flour and stir over low heat for 2 to 3 minutes. Do not brown the roux.

Add the mushrooms to the onion mixture. Cover and cook over low heat for 10 minutes, or until the mushrooms are tender but not limp. Stir occasionally. Gradually add asparagus-stock mixture, stirring constantly for 3 to 5 minutes, or until the mixture is smooth.

Add the cream and garlic salt, heat through, but do not boil. Garnish with fresh parsley. Yield: 4-6 servings.

From: **Elsah's Landing
Restaurant**
18 La Salle Street
Elsah

Chicken Curry Soup

1 chicken, cut up
6 peppercorns
2 ribs celery
1 medium onion, peeled
4 cups water
1 medium onion, finely diced
1 cup finely diced carrots
¼ cup butter
2 teaspoons curry powder
2 tablespoons cornstarch
¼ cup water
2 teaspoons salt
¼ teaspoon sugar
1 cup light cream
　(half & half)
apple slices

Combine the chicken, peppercorns, celery, and onion with water in a large saucepan. Cover and simmer for 1 hour, or until chicken and vegetables are tender. Cool. Remove the chicken from skin and bones, cut into bite-size pieces and set aside. Discard skin and bones. Remove and strain liquid for stock.

Sauté onion and carrots in butter in medium saucepan over low heat for 5 minutes, or until onion is golden but not brown. Add the curry powder and sauté for an additional 10 minutes. Add reserved stock, bring to a simmer and cook over medium heat for 5 minutes.

Mix the cornstarch with the quarter cup of water and stir this into the simmering stock. Add the salt, sugar and reserved chicken. Add the cream, heat through, but do not boil. Adjust seasoning to taste. Garnish each serving with an apple slice. Yield: 4-6 servings.

From:　**Elsah's Landing
Restaurant**
18 La Salle Street
Elsah

Clam Chowder Sauron

1 cup diced onion
1 cup diced potato
olive oil, butter
2 cups fresh clams
2 cups fish stock
　or clam juice
1 cup milk
1 cup half & half cream
1 cup dry white wine
pinch saffron
pinch white pepper
1 bay leaf

Sauté the onions and potatoes in a little olive oil and butter for 10 minutes. Remove and set aside. Sauté the clams for 5 minutes. Remove. Deglaze the pan with the white wine.

In the meantime, bring the fish stock/clam juice and milk to a simmer and then add the half & half. Add the deglazed white wine to this mixture, then add the clams, potatoes and onions. Add the saffron, white pepper and bay leaf. Simmer over low heat for ½ to ¾ of an hour. Remove the bay leaf, adjust the seasoning and serve. You may add a bit of cornstarch if you wish your chowder thickened.

From:　　　**Cafe du Louvre**
16 East Main Street
East Dundee

Washington Clam Chowder

1 ounce bacon, diced
4 ounces butter
4 ounces diced onion
4 ounces diced celery
3 ounces diced green pepper
3 ounces flour
1 gallon chicken stock
2 pounds potatoes, diced
1¼ pounds frozen corn
½ can (#10) tomatoes
⅜ ounce baking soda
thyme to taste
basil to taste
salt and white pepper
   to taste
1½ teaspoons sugar
1 (48 ounce) can clams
1½ quarts half and half

Sauté the bacon in the butter in a heavy stockpot. Add the onion, celery and green pepper. Cook until tender, do not brown. Add the flour and stir, cooking for a few minutes, but do not brown. Pour in the chicken stock, add the potatoes and the corn. Bring to a simmer and then add the tomatoes, baking soda, herbs and sugar. Last add the clams and simmer until everything is tender. Add the cream just before serving. Yield: approximately 2 gallons.

From: **Central Station Cafe**
220 East Front Street
Bloomington

Corn Chowder

5 tablespoons unsalted butter
2 red bell peppers, cored, seeded
   and cut into ¼-inch dice
½ cup sliced wild mushrooms,
   (shitake and oyster for example)
6 scallions, sliced
kernels from 8 ears of corn
2 tomatoes, peeled, seeded
   and diced
8 cups chicken stock
salt to taste
freshly ground pepper
chopped fresh herbs

Melt the butter in a skillet. Add the peppers, wild mushrooms and scallions and sauté until tender. Add the corn, cover, and simmer until tender. In a large soup pot, combine the sautéed ingredients with the tomatoes and the chicken stock. Bring to a boil and simmer until reduced by one third to one half. Coarsely puree one half the soup, one cup at a time. Combine this puree with the remaining soup. Reduce further if desired. Season to taste with salt, pepper and herbs of your choice. Yield: 4 servings.

From: **Melange Restaurant**
1515 Sheridan, Plaza del Lago
Wilmette

Mushroom Burgundy Soup

½ pound mushrooms with stems
4 tablespoons butter
2 tablespoons flour
1 cup chicken stock
1 cup good Burgundy
1 cup cream
½ teaspoon Worcestershire
   sauce
salt and pepper to taste

Dice the mushrooms into ¼-inch pieces and sauté in 2 tablespoons of the butter, set aside. In the remaining butter mix the flour and cook over a medium heat stirring constantly until light brown in color. Add the chicken stock and boil for 5 minutes. Then add the cream and Worcesterchire sauce and bring back to a boil, add the mushrooms and season to taste with salt and pepper.

If you wish a thicker soup, an additional roux may be made with another 2 tablespoons of flour and 2 tablespoons of butter. Whisk into the soup until the desired consistency is reached. Yield: 4-6 servings.

From: **Le Radis Rouge/
Jumer's Chateau**
Jumer's Drive
Bloomington

French Onion Soup

4 pounds yellow onions
¼ cup margarine
¼ cup sugar
⅝ cup flour
¾ teaspoon white pepper
1 tablespoon paprika
1 bay leaf
½ cup dry white wine
6 cups beef stock
½ teaspoon Kitchen Bouquet

Peel and slice onions into rings. In a heavy skillet or saucepan sauté the onions with the margarine for 30 minutes, then sprinkle with the sugar. Sauté the onions another 30 minutes stirring to caramelize evenly.

Sprinkle with the flour, cook another 10 minutes then add the white pepper, paprika, bay leaf, white wine, beef stock and Kitchen Bouquet. Cook over low heat for approximately 1 hour, stirring occasionally.

To serve place a slice of French bread or a handful of croutons in crockery bowls. Ladle the soup over the bread, top with mozzarella cheese and place under broiler for a few seconds. Yield: 6-12 servings.

From:

**Cindi's Cafe
& Catering**
222 South 9th Street
Mount Vernon

Smoked Pheasant Consommé

bones from 1
  smoked pheasant
1 gallon water
1 tablespoon fresh
  chopped parsley
1 medium onion
1 carrot, diced
1 stalk celery, diced
1 yellow turnip, diced
meat from ½ smoked
  pheasant
2 bay leaves
3 tablespoons butter
½ cup sherry

Brown the pheasant bones in the oven at 350 degrees, turning to brown on all sides.

Put the bones in the water. Add the peelings and trimmings of the vegetables and simmer for 3 hours. Strain.

Sauté the vegetables, pheasant meat, bay leaves in butter until tender. Add the sherry and reduce to cook out alcohol. Add the vegetable meat mixture to the stock. Season to taste with salt and pepper.

From: **Eagle Ridge Inn
          & Resort**
          Highway 20 East
          Galena

Chilled Peachy Blueberry Soup

 6 ripe peaches
¾ cup orange juice
1¼ teaspoons tapioca
1 cup buttermilk
⅛ teaspoon allspice
⅛ teaspoon cinnamon
½ cup sugar
1 tablespoon lemon juice
1 teaspoon grated lemon rind
½ cup blueberries

Peel and halve the peaches, removing the pits. Cut in quarters and combine with orange juice in the blender or food processor. Puree.

Mix tapioca with ¼ cup of peach mixture. Put into a small saucepan and add the remaining peach mixture. Heat, stirring until mixture comes to a boil. Cook one minute or until thickened. Pour into medium bowl.

Add buttermilk, allspice, cinnamon, sugar, lemon juice and grated rind. Mix well. Chill.

Just before serving, add whole blueberries. Season to taste. Yield: 4 servings.

From: **Elsah's Landing Restaurant**
18 La Salle Street
Elsah

Sweet and Sour Cabbage Soup

12 cups shredded
  and diced cabbage
2 onions, chopped
6 cups beef broth
6 cups chicken broth
4 cooked potatoes, chopped
2-3 cups chopped cooked meat*
1 teaspoon crushed garlic
½ teaspoon thyme
½ teaspoon ground allspice
2 teaspoons cayenne
salt to taste
2 cup chopped tomatoes
½ cup tomato paste
¼ cup brown sugar
¼ cup cider vinegar
¼ cup lemon juice

*Smoked sausage, ham, beef,
pork roast, pot roast are all good
used in this soup.

Simmer cabbage and onions in the broth until tender, about ½ hour. Add the potatoes, meat, spices, etc. and heat through. This soup improves on the second day as the flavors have a chance to meld.

This makes a lot of soup and it freezes well. At the restaurant it usually sells out quickly.

From:

**The Mansion
at Golconda**
Columbus Street
Golconda

Meat & Poultry

Meat & Poultry

Meat and poultry remain one of the mainstays of any cookbook, whatever the latest food trend. People who like to cook and like to eat are always interested in new ways of preparing the standbys.

Here from Illinois chefs are some wonderful new ways to prepare chicken, veal, beef and even a recipe for squab. Read, try them and enjoy them; they are delicious!

Chicken Albufera

4 whole boned chicken breasts
proscuitto or country smoked ham
stuffing
string for tying
fresh broccoli

Stuffing:
2 cups shredded, day-old bread
¼ cup finely minced onion
¼ cup sesame seeds
milk
1-2 teaspoons hickory salt
1 egg, beaten

Sauce:
¾ cup olive oil
2 cups chopped onions
3 green peppers, chopped
2 cups sliced mushrooms
3 garlic cloves, minced
3 pounds tomatoes, skinned
   and diced or crushed
½ teaspoon ground cloves
1½ cups rose wine
2 pints tomato juice
½ pound honey
¾ cup yellow mustard
1½ tablespoons minced parsley

The sauce should be prepared a day ahead in order to let the flavors blend properly. Sauté the onions, peppers, mushrooms and garlic in the olive oil. When the garlic browns slightly add all the other ingredients and simmer for about 30 minutes. The sauce should be reduced slightly. Pour into a storage container and refrigerate overnight. The tomatoes, peppers and mushrooms should remain firm and intact. The taste should be slightly sweet, but tangy from the mustard.

Mix the stuffing ingredients together, adding the beaten egg with enough milk to moisten the stuffing.

Lay out the boned chicken breasts. Pound each one to flatten slightly. Lay a slice of the ham over each breast. Place a bit of the stuffing in the center of the chicken. Wrap one end of the chicken over the stuffing, then wrap the other end. Tie the chicken with the string, so that it binds the chicken around the ham and stuffing.

Put water in a large, heavy bottomed saucepan. For each quart of water, add a cup of white wine. Bring to a boil, add the chicken breasts. Cook for 22 minutes, or until done. While the chicken is cooking, prepare the sauce for serving, which should take 5 minutes.

Cook the broccoli until it is just fork tender. Keep warm.

Heat the sauce in a shallow pan until the sauce just bubbles. Make a roux of flour and butter, adding a bit at a time, just until the sauce thickens slightly. Turn off the heat and cover for about 3 minutes to allow the roux to blend.

Put the chicken breasts on a plate with the broccoli alongside. Pour the sauce over the chicken and serve garnished with lemon slices. Yield: 4-6 servings.

From: **The Kingston Inn**
300 North Main Street
Galena

Chicken Breasts with Cheese and Artichokes
Grilled Corn/Spinach Noodles

4 chicken breasts,
  boned and skinned
1/3 cup virgin olive oil
1 cup shredded Gruyère cheese
1 (8½ ounce) can artichoke
  hearts, finely chopped
2 whole lemons
salt and white pepper to taste

Noodles:
1 pound fresh spinach noodles
½ cup virgin olive oil
salt and white pepper to taste

Grilled Corn:
2 sticks margarine
1 large red bell pepper,
  chopped fine
2 bunches scallions, chopped fine
1 stick unsalted butter
1 2-pound bag frozen corn kernels
salt and white pepper to taste
watercress

Preheat the oven to 350 degrees. For the chicken, salt and pepper the breasts, cut a slit 2 inches wide in the center of each breast. Heat the olive oil in a large skillet over medium heat. Sauté the breast until brown on each side. Remove from the skillet. Stuff cheese and artichokes into each breast. Squeeze the juice from the lemons, rub on the breasts. Bake on a sheet pan until tender. Remove, pour the rest of the lemon juice over the breasts, keep warm.

In a large saucepan or stockpot, boil water for the spinach noodles. Add the olive oil, then the noodles. Cook al dente, remove and drain. Add a little oil, salt and pepper to taste.

Melt the margarine in a cast iron skillet. Cook the red bell pepper until tender for about 5 minutes. Add the scallions and cook for 3 minutes. Add salt and pepper. Remove. Add the butter and then add the corn. Cook until browned. Remove from the skillet, mixing all the ingredients together.

Put the corn mixture together with the noodles and serve topped with the chicken breasts, garnish with watercress. Yield: 4 servings.

From: **Rockford Woman's Club Food Shop**
2405 North Church Street
Rockford

Chicken Monterey

4 whole chicken breasts, skinned, boned
1 stick butter
¼ teaspoon basil
¼ teaspoon white pepper
¾ teaspoon oregano
¾ teaspoon marjoram
¾ teaspoon parsley
½ teaspoon salt
¼ pound Monterey Jack cheese, cut into 8 cubes
¾ cup flour
2 eggs, beaten
1½ cups bread crumbs, white and whole wheat
1 cup sauterne

Preheat the oven to 350 degrees. Pound the chicken breasts until very thin. Cut in half to form two equal size pieces.

Whip butter until fluffy. Add the herbs, mix well and divide in half.

Using one half the butter mixture, place approximately 1 tablespoon of mixture in the center of each breast half. Top with one cube of cheese. Roll up, tucking the ends in.

Roll chicken pieces in flour, dip into the beaten eggs and then roll in the bread crumbs. Place in a greased casserole.

Using the other half of the butter mixture, top each chicken roll with a dollop of butter. Bake in the oven for 20 minutes. Pour the wine over the chicken and bake an additional 20 minutes. Baste occasionally.

Very good served with a parmesan fettucine and lightly steamed vegetables.

From:

Cindi's Cafe and Catering
2222 South 9th Street
Mount Vernon

Chicken Piccata

6 6-ounce boneless
   chicken breasts
6 eggs, beaten
3 cups freshly grated
   parmesan cheese
6 tablespoons lemon butter

Lemon butter:
¼ pound butter
⅛ cup caper juice
⅛ cup white wine
1 teaspoon fresh lemon juice
1 teaspoon capers
1 teaspoon fines herbes
¼ teaspoon white pepper

Preheat oven to 350 degrees. Dip the chicken breasts in beaten eggs, then roll in the parmesan cheese until well covered. Place in a buttered baking dish. Bake in the oven for approximately 10 minutes or until done. Add the lemon butter and cook for another minute or two. Serve with fettucine alfredo. Yield: 6 servings.

To make the lemon butter, simply whip the butter until creamy, then add in the other ingredients, blending well.

From: **The Rockwell Inn**
2400 West Route 6
Morris

Poulet Sauté aux Poireaux
et Crème de Basil

3 chickens, approximately
   2 pounds each
butter
1 pound leeks,
   cleaned and julienned

Sauce:
3 tablespoons butter
2 tablespoons shallots
½ cup VSOP cognac*
1 cup dry white wine
3 cups chicken stock
2 cups heavy cream
1 tomato, chopped
10 fresh basil leaves
salt and pepper

*VSOP is a designation used by
the distillers of cognac and simply
means Very Superior Old Pale.
This is one of the best grades of
cognac and it would be permissa-
ble to use plain cognac to flame
the sauce.

Bone the chicken and sauté in butter. Place in the oven and bake at 400 degrees for 15 minutes.

Remove the chicken and set aside. Sauté julienne of leek in pan juices, butter mixture for 5 minutes and remove. Next, sauté the shallots until transparent.

Add the cognac, flame and reduce. Add wine and reduce. Add the chicken stock and reduce to ¼ cup.

Add the cream and boil for 2 minutes. Add the diced tomato, basil leaves, and leeks. Season to taste with salt and pepper.

To serve, nap the chicken with the sauce. Yield: 6 servings.

From: **Le Titi de Paris**
1015 West Dundee Road
Arlington Heights

Sautéed Chicken with Rice Pilaf

2 boneless chicken breasts
1 large onion, diced
1 green pepper
1 red bell pepper
butter

Marinade:
½ cup olive oil
½ cup fresh lemon juice
½ cup chablis
1-2 cloves garlic, crushed
salt and pepper to taste

Rice Pilaf:
½ cup fine noodles
2 tablespoons butter
1 cup rice
2 cups water with bouillon cube or
   2 cups good chicken stock

Prepare the marinade by combining all the ingredients in a non-reactive or glass bowl or dish. Cut the chicken into 2-inch bite-size pieces and marinate for at least 4 hours.

Dice the onion, green and red peppers into bite-size pieces. In a stainless steel sauté pan, melt 2-3 tablespoons butter over medium high heat. Add the pieces of chicken, the onion, and the peppers. Sauté quickly over high heat just until done, vegetables should still be slightly crisp. Serve with rice pilaf.

Brown the noodles in the butter. Add the rice and stir to coat with the butter. When all the rice is coated with the butter, add the chicken stock or the water and bouillon cube. Boil until rice is cooked, then cover and allow to steam for a few minutes to fluff the rice. Serve.

From:

Sayat Nova
20 West Golf Road
Des Plaines

Grilled Cornish Hen
with Cranberry Garlic Sauce

6 fresh or frozen cornish hens

Marinade:
2 cups peanut oil
1 cup balsamic vinegar
3 teaspoons salt
2 teaspoons black pepper
1 tablespoon tarragon
1 tablespoon basil
1 tablespoon oregano

Cranberry Garlic Sauce:
8 ounces cranberry vinegar
4 cup chardonnay wine
8 tablespoons cranberry liqueur
12 tablespoons sautéed shallots
10 whole, peeled garlic cloves
2 quarts chicken stock
cornstarch
water
1 cup fresh sautéed mushrooms
1 cup fresh cranberries
½ cup cranberry liqueur

Split open the cornish hens from the back, removing the backbone and flattening with the bottom of a heavy pan.

Blend together all the ingredients of the marinade and marinate the hens for 1-2 hours. Grill the birds, turning frequently, until the juices run clear, about 10-15 minutes.

Place the cranberry vinegar, chardonnay, cranberry liqueur, shallots and garlic in a heavy bottomed saucepan and reduce by half. Add the chicken stock and again reduce by half.

Blend together a little cornstarch and water and add to the sauce to thicken. Add the mushrooms, cranberries and the cranberry liqueur and bring to a simmer. Serve over the grilled cornish hens. Yield: 6 servings.

From: **The Public Landing Restaurant**
200 West 8th Street
Lockport

Pigeonneaux à Sauce L'Ail
Boned Squab with Garlic Sauce

6 14-ounce squab, livers reserved
salt and freshly ground pepper
7 tablespoons unsalted butter
36 unpeeled garlic cloves
½ cup dry white wine
½ cup chicken stock,
   preferably homemade
3 tablespoons brandy
24 medium mushrooms, trimmed
chicken quenelles

Have the butcher bone squabs without cutting them open. This is called clove boning—or do it yourself following directions at the end of this recipe. Remove all bones for making stock. Season squab lightly with salt and pepper. Preheat oven to 450 degrees. Melt 4 tablespoons butter in a large ovenproof skillet over medium-high heat. Add squab and sauté until browned on all sides. Add garlic and brown quickly. Transfer to oven and roast, basting occasionally, until squab is done, about 20-25 minutes. Transfer squab and garlic to serving platter and keep warm.

Deglaze the skillet with the wine. Peel 12 cloves of garlic and crush them with the flat of a large knife. Add to the skillet. Melt 1 tablespoon of butter in a small skillet over medium heat. Add the reserved livers and sauté until evenly browned but still pink inside. Transfer to food processor or blender and puree to paste. Add a bit of the wine mixture and blend well. Stir livers back into remaining wine mixture. Add stock and brandy, place pan over low heat and simmer until the sauce is heated through. Meanwhile melt the remaining 2 tablespoons of butter in large skillet over medium heat. Add the mushrooms and sauté until golden. Pour sauce over squab and garnish platter with mushrooms, remaining garlic cloves and chicken quenelles. Serve immediately.

Chicken Quenelles:
1 pound boned and
   skinned chicken breasts
1 teaspoon salt
½ teaspoon freshly ground pepper
¼ teaspoon freshly ground
   nutmeg
2 egg whites, lightly beaten
2 cups whipping/heavy cream
hot salted water or chicken stock

Grind chicken finely in food processor or with meat grinder. Add the salt, pepper and nutmeg and blend well. Gradually add the egg whites, mixing vigorously after each addition. Gradually add cream and mix until mixture is firm. Dip 2 teaspoons into boiling water. Heap some of the chicken mixture onto 1 spoon and round it off with the second spoon. Dip the second spoon in hot water again, slip it under oval and slide quenelle into buttered skillet. Repeat until quenelles line skillet in single layer, but do not crowd them. Slowly add enough hot salted water or stock to float quenelles. Bring liquid to a simmer over low heat and poach quenelles until firm, about 5 to 10 minutes, but do not boil. Remove with a slotted spoon and drain well on paper towels. Yield: 6 dozen small quenelles, about 6 servings.

How to bone a squab: A sharp boning knife and scissors are needed. Flash freeze the squab until some ice crystals are formed. Clean out cavity. Rinse bird under cold water and pat dry with paper towels. Trim wings at joint, discarding tips. Stand the bird upright. Using a sharp knife cut through wings where they join the body. Loosen the meat and carcass along the keel bone and pushing against the bone towards the bottom. You may want to scrape with the knife from time to time instead of using your fingers. Do not be concerned if small bits of meat come away from the skin since any small pieces can be returned to the cavity after boning. Turn bird over onto breast and carefully loosen meat from back by pushing with fingers or scraping with knife. Gradually turn skin inside out as you work. Cut thigh bones from joints using scissors and discard the carcass. Turn bird skin side out, feeling for any small bones you may have missed, discard.

From: **Le Francais**
269 South Milwaukee Street
Wheeling

Grilled Filet of Beef
in Lobster Cream Sauce

6 8- to 10-ounce filets of beef

Lobster Cream Sauce:
1 cup lobster meat
clarified butter
7 egg yolks
juice of ½ lemon
¼ cup balsamic vinegar
2 tablespoons tarragon
4 tablespoons sauteed shallots
½ tablespoon basil

To prepare the sauce, sauté the lobster meat in clarified butter until lightly browned.

Place the egg yolks, lemon juice, vinegar, tarragon, shallots, and basil in the food processor and process. Add the lobster and process.

With the processor running, slowly add the butter in a steady stream.

Grill the filets according to desired degree of doneness and serve with the

*6 sticks unsalted butter
melted and clarified*

sauce, accompanied by potatoes and fresh vegetables.

From: **Tallgrass Restaurant**
1006 South State Street
Lockport

Medallions of Beef
with Zinfandel Sauce

*12 4-ounce beef tenderloin
medallions
1 bottle good zinfandel
1 cup demiglace*
red champagne grapes
for garnish*

*To prepare a demiglace use a strong beef stock made from browned beef bones, carrots, onions, celery, tomatoes, bay leaves, parsley, cloves, black peppercorns and red wine. After simmering for at least 8 hours, strain, add tomato paste, and reduce by half. Thicken with a brown roux and finish with sherry. Season to taste with salt and pepper.

Reduce the zinfandel over low heat, stirring occasionally, until it thickens somewhat and is reduced so that only 1 cup remains.

Combine the reduced zinfandel and the demiglace and simmer another 15 minutes.

Grill the beef medallions to desired doneness. Put sauce on serving plate and place medallions on top of sauce. Garnish with tiny champagne grapes. This dish goes well with herbed tomato pasta and red cabbage sauteed with Grand Marnier. Yield: 6 servings.

From: **Eagle Ridge Inn
& Resort**
Highway 20 East
Galena

Steak Diane

½ pound butter
6 ribs celery, sliced
18 green onions, sliced
16 fresh mushrooms, sliced
6 8-ounce filets, sliced
   into 3 medallions each
dash Worcestershire sauce
dash soy sauce
salt and freshly ground pepper
   to taste
4 cups bordelaise sauce

Bordelaise Sauce:
½ pound butter
1 onion, chopped
1 pound fresh mushrooms
½ cup flour
1 cup Burgundy
1 cup au jus
1 clove garlic, chopped
1 bay leaf
pinch fresh pepper
pinch of celery salt
pinch salt
2 dashes soy sauce
Kitchen Bouquet to color

For the bordelaise sauce: Melt the butter, sauté the onions until transparent; add mushrooms which you have chopped, cook until tender; add flour and cook for 2 minutes; add wine while stirring constantly; add au jus and cook until smooth. Add the garlic and seasonings. Simmer for 15 minutes, add the Kitchen Bouquet if necessary for color.

Now melt the butter, add the celery, green onions, mushrooms, sauté until tender. Do not overcook. Add the filet medallions, top with Worcestershire, top the vegetables with the soy sauce. Add the salt and freshly ground pepper. Cook the medallions to desired degree of doneness, then add the bordelaise and heat through. Flame with brandy and serve. Yield: 6 servings.

From: **The Red Door Inn**
1701 Water Street
Peru

Steak Dijon

The chef at The Mansion came up with this recipe for a customer who complained that Sauce Bearnaise was too sweet.

6 6-ounce beef tenderloin
   medallions trimmed and
   flattened to 1 inch
2 tablespoons butter
2 tablespoons garlic oil

Sauce:
2 tablespoons minced scallions
2 tablespoons butter
2 tablespoons beef stock
⅓ cup dry white wine
1 cup heavy cream
1 tablespoon minced parsley
2 tablespoons Dijon-style
   mustard
⅛ teaspoon thyme
2 teaspoons green peppercorns,
   rinsed and drained

To make garlic oil take 1 quart vegetable oil and place 1 clove garlic, peeled and cut in half in the oil. Allow to steep long enough for the garlic to flavor the oil.

For the sauce, sauté the scallions in 1 tablespoon of the butter and 2 tablespoons of the beef stock. Add the wine and reduce to 2 tablespoons. Add the cream and boil until thickened and syrupy—about 10 minutes over a medium high flame. Whisk in the mustard, thyme and peppercorns.

Heat a heavy cast iron skillet to red-hot. Combine the butter and garlic oil and brush on the bottom of the skillet. It will smoke. Sear the medallions to desired doneness—about 1 minute per side for rare, an additional minute per side for each degree of doneness. Top each medallion with 2 tablespoons of the sauce. Yield: 6 servings.

From:

**The Mansion
at Golconda**
Columbus Street
Golconda

Rack of Lamb
Diable a la Dijonnaise

*1 rack of spring lamb
  (about 2½ pounds)
2 tablespoons butter
5 ounces Dijon-style mustard
6 ounces bread crumbs
1½ tablespoons finely
  chopped garlic
4 tablespoons chopped
  fresh parsley
½ teaspoon salt
½ teaspoon freshly ground
  black pepper*

Sauce Provençal:
*1 tablespoon chopped shallot
1½ stick butter
1 teaspoon chopped garlic
¼ cup chopped parsley*

Preheat the oven to 450 degrees. After you have trimmed the fat from the rack of lamb, sprinkle it with salt and pepper. Melt 2 tablespoons of butter in a skillet and brown the meat on all sides over medium high heat about 5-10 minutes. Place the lamb in the oven for 15 minutes.

Remove the lamb from the oven and trim off all remaining fat with a sharp knife. Combine the mustard, bread crumbs, garlic, and parsley with more salt and pepper, if desired, and spread over the surface of the lamb. Return the lamb to the oven for 10 minutes for medium rare. If you like the meat well done, cook 10-15 minutes more.

Take the rack from the oven and let the meat rest for 10 minutes in a lukewarm place before carving. Make the sauce by combining all the ingredients in a heavy bottomed pan and heating just to a simmer.

Holding the meat on the flat side with a cooking fork, cut chops by slicing between the ribs. Serve with garniture of vegetables and potatoes with the sauce on top of the lamb ribs. A good bottle of Beaujolais or Cote du Rhone goes well with this dish. Bon Appetit! Yield: 2 servings.

From: **Cafe du Louvre**
16 East Main Street
East Dundee

Pork Cordon Nikkolette

1 pound pork loin, trimmed
4 ounces cooked lobster
4 tablespoons almonds,
   lightly toasted
2 ounces butter
salt and pepper to taste
2 ounces flour
2 eggs with 1 tablespoon water
2 ounces fine bread crumbs

Sauce:
½ quart heavy cream
1 chicken bouillon cube
1½ ounces pina colada schnapps
dash of curaçao

Cut the pork loin into four 4-ounce slices and pound flat without tearing the meat. Distribute the lobster, almonds and butter evenly onto the flattened pork. Sprinkle with seasonings and roll up the pork, sealing in all the ingredients. Wrap in plastic wrap and refrigerate for 6 hours. Preheat oven to 350 degrees. Remove the plastic wrap and roll in flour, then in egg wash, then in bread crumbs. Sauté in butter until light brown and place in the oven for 20 minutes.

In a heavy bottomed saucepan reduce the cream by $2/3$ and dissolve the chicken bouillon cube in it. When about to boil, add the pina colada schnapps and curaçao liqueur. Blend together until heated through.

Slice the pork crosswise, layer on a plate and nap with the sauce. Yield: 4 servings.

From: **Le Radis Rouge/
          Jumer's Chateau**
          Jumer Road
          Bloomington

Filet de Veau
au Cresson et Chèvre
Tenderloin of Veal
with Watercress and Goat Cheese

24 ounces veal tenderloin,
   trimmed to 4-ounce slices
10 ounces mushrooms, pureed
2 shallots, chopped
6 ounces veal tips, ground
4 tablespoons butter
3 ounces chèvre (goat cheese)

Sauce:
12 ounces finely chopped
   veal trimmings
2 tablespoons butter
1 small carrot, diced
1 small onion, diced
1 shallot, diced
1 rib celery, diced
1 garlic clove, minced
3 cups chicken stock
2 cups heavy cream
1 cup fresh watercress,
   blanched and pureed

Begin the sauce; sauté the veal trimmings in 2 tablespoons butter until well browned. Add all vegetables and quickly add the stock. Simmer for 40 minutes, stirring occasionally. Strain, remove vegetables and trimmings. Reduce to 4 tablespoons liquid.

Add the cream and bring to a boil. Just before fininshing sauce, whisk in pureed watercress.

Pound flat the veal portions. Make a slit lengthwise in center of each portion for the stuffing. Set aside.

Sauté the pureed mushrooms with shallot and veal tips in 2 tablespoons butter until dry. Stuff each veal portion with the veal mushroom stuffing. Sauté 6-8 minutes in remaining 2 tablespoons butter until lightly browned, but still pink inside.

Serve with noodles, nap with the sauce and sprinkle the crumbled chevre on top.

From: **Le Titi de Paris**
          1015 West Dundee Road
          Arlington Heights

Veal Merissa

12 slices veal loin, 2 ounces each
½ cup flour
salt and pepper to taste
¼ cup olive oil
½ cup cream sherry
⅓ cup dry white wine
2 minced shallots
2 cups heavy cream
fresh vegetable garnish

Place the slices of veal on a cutting board. Cover the slices with plastic wrap and pound with the flat side of heavy knife or meat mallet to ¼-inch thickness. Trim pieces into desired shapes. Dredge slices in the flour seasoned with the salt and pepper. Heat 2 tablespoons of the olive oil in a skillet. Add a few pieces of the veal. Cook over medium high heat for 2 minutes on each side or until brown. Remove from skillet. Add remaining 2 tablespoons olive oil to skillet. Cook remaining veal. Add cream sherry and dry white wine to skillet. Bring to a boil slowly and again reduce by half. Season with additional sherry and salt and pepper. Strain and keep warm. Spoon sauce on plate and place scallops of veal into the sauce. Garnish with scallion rings, cherry tomato roses or any fresh vegetables of your choice. Yield: 4 servings.

From: **Le Radis Rouge/**
          Jumer's Chateau
          Jumer Road
          Bloomington

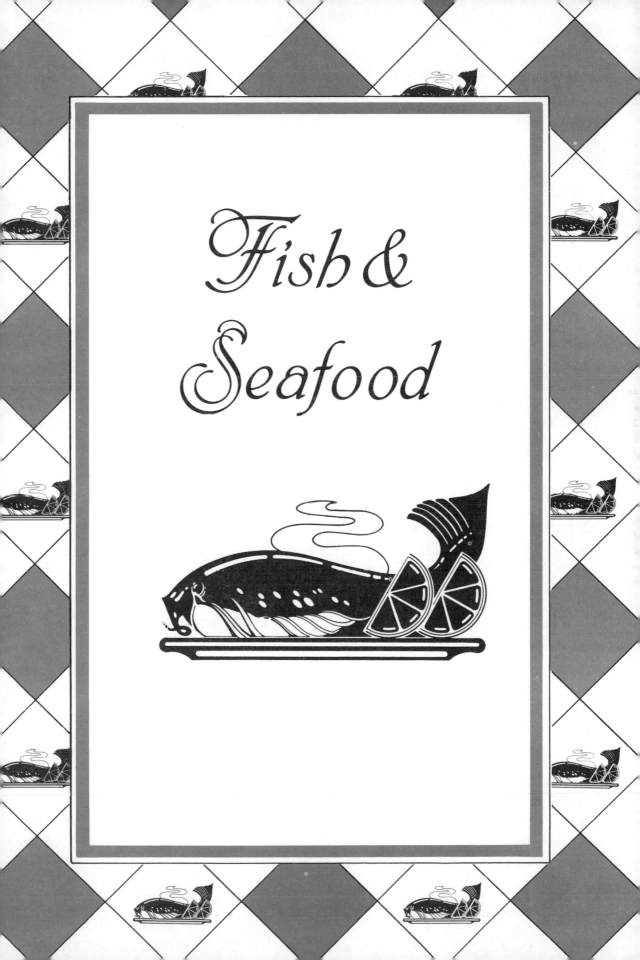

Fish & Seafood

Fish & Seafood

Perhaps the largest growth in the field of cooking in the United States has been in our handling of fish and seafood. No longer content with the simple ways we prepared it in the past, we have adopted and adapted the traditional ways with seafoods of other countries. We have also come up with new and imaginative ways of our own.

We have rediscovered our own fish, like catfish, and new and delectable ways of preparing them. Here, from Illinois chefs are some of the best.

Besugo a la Basque

Enough light, flaky fish filets
   such as Red Snapper, Pollack,
   or Bream to serve 4-6
¼ cup crushed fresh garlic
1 cup rose wine
½ teaspoon basil
3-4 pounds fresh tomatoes
12 ounces tomato juice*
¼ teaspoon salt
¼ cup fresh lemon juice,
   seeds removed
1 tablespoon white pepper
¼-½ cup fresh minced parsley
2-4 cups chopped onions,
   as desired
¼ cup olive oil
6-12 diced olives (optional)

*This amount will vary depend-
ing on the juiciness of the fresh
tomatoes.

In a heavy stockpot, sauté the onions in the olive oil until wilted. Add all the other ingredients, except the fish and simmer for 30 minutes, until the sauce is well blended. Cover and place in the refrigerator for several hours or overnight. Reheat just before serving. Preheat oven to 375 degrees. In oven-proof pan, place olive oil or butter to grease bottom. Add fish filets on top, pour some of the heated sauce on top and place in the oven for 25 minutes or until fish is done. Serve from the oven over a bed of rice or with crispy toast made from a good French or Spanish bread.

One of my favorite pan toast recipes is: slice thick cross sections from a long baguette (French bread). Fill a shallow pan with olive oil about ½-inch deep. When the oil is very hot, almost smoking, carefully lay the pieces of bread in the oil, turning quickly as they toast. Drain on paper towels.

From: **The Kingston Inn**
300 North Main Street
Galena

Catfish Almaden

When this dish was developed, an Almaden wine was used but any good dry sherry makes the dish what it is!

4 tablespoons melted butter
4 pounds catfish fillets
¼ teaspoon thyme
¼ teaspoon marjoram
1 teaspoon dried parsley
pinch nutmeg
½ teaspoon tarragon
1 tablespoon chicken base
  (bouillon granules)
2 cups dry sherry
½ cup chopped parsley
½ cup chopped green onions

Preheat oven to 375 degrees. Generously butter the bottom of a baking dish, place the fillets in the dish. Mix the herbs and chicken bouillon granules together, whisk in the sherry. Heat sherry and herbs until nearly boiling. Pour over the fish. Mix the parsley and onions and layer evenly over the fish. Bake for 12-15 minutes or until the fish is opaque and flakes easily when tested with a fork. Yield 6 servings.

From:

**The Mansion
at Golconda**
Columbus Street
Golconda

Grilled Mississippi Catfish
with Roasted Sweet Red Pepper Relish

3 red peppers
2 shallots, peeled and diced
1 clove garlic, chopped
butter
1 ounce port wine
1 ounce red raspberry vinegar
salt and pepper to taste
2 tablespoons oil
1 teaspoon fresh lemon juice
½ teaspoon seasoning salt
4 8-ounce catfish filets
lime wheel or garlic bud
  for garnish

Start a charcoal fire and let it burn down to red coals. Roast the red peppers whole on the grill, preferably with the lid on, until blackened and shriveled slightly. Turn the peppers so they roast evenly on all sides.

Peel the tough, clear outer skin of the peppers, removing all the blackened peel. Then cut in half and remove the seeds, membranes and stem. Chop the peppers in small pieces or put in the food processor or blender for a few seconds.

Sauté the shallots and chopped garlic in butter. Add the port, raspberry vinegar and reduce. Add the red peppers and simmer for 10 minutes. Season to taste with salt and pepper.

Combine the oil, fresh lemon juice and seasoning salt and dredge the fish in the oil mixture. Grill the fish over the coals for about 3 minutes on a side. Before serving, spoon a strip of the red pepper relish over the fish. Garnish with a grilled lime wheel or roasted garlic bud. Yield: 4 servings.

From: **Eagle Ridge Inn & Resort**
Highway 20 East
Galena

Cioppino Espanola

Cioppino was introduced to this country by Portugese sailors, but the basic dish is shared by both Spain and Portugal.

2 cups chopped onions
2-3 green peppers, diced
2 cups sliced fresh mushrooms
olive oil
1-2 garlic cloves, crushed
3-4 pounds fresh skinned
   tomatoes
½ teaspoon ground cloves
1-2 cups rose wine
2 tablespoons freshly chopped
   parsley
½ teaspoon cayenne
salt and pepper to taste
fresh shelled shrimp, clams,
   mussels, shelled scallops,
   crabmeat, fresh fish

Sauté the onions, green peppers, and mushrooms in the olive oil. Add the garlic as the onions begin to wilt slightly. When garlic is lightly browned, remove from the heat.

Put the rest of the ingredients, except the fish, with the onion mixture in a large stock-pot. Simmer for about 30 minutes. Cool overnight, allowing the flavors to blend.

After the sauce has cooled overnight, bring back to a quick boil, adding the fish and sea-food of your choice. The quick boil will cook the seafood. Then serve over rice, garnished with lemon slices and fresh parsley sprigs.

Diced olives and a few tablespoons of dry sherry may be added, if you desire. They should be added after the sauce has been allowed to sit overnight, otherwise they change the basic flavor structure too much. Yield: 6-8 servings.

From: **The Kingston Inn**
             300 North Main Street
             Galena

Lobster in Vanilla Sauce

1 carrot, rough chopped
1 large onion, rough chopped
1 rib celery, rough chopped
8-10 parsley stems

Put the vegetables, the herbs, peppercorns and garlic in the fish stock in a heavy stock-pot and bring to a boil. Simmer for an hour. Then add the vanilla bean and the white wine

2 bay leaves
¼ teaspoon tarragon
¼ teaspoon thyme
salt to taste
4-5 black peppercorns
1 garlic clove
½ gallon fish stock or water
1 vanilla bean, sliced in half
½ gallon white wine
2-3 branches seaweed
2 lobsters, 1½ pounds each

Vanilla sauce:
3-4 shallots, chopped
½ teaspoon butter
¼ cup white wine
1 vanilla bean, chopped
1 quart heavy cream
1 ounce fish glace
1 pound bay scallops
salt and pepper to taste

Leek garnish:
1 leek, chopped
1 tablespoon butter
6 ounces heavy cream
salt and pepper to taste

and bring back to a boil. Add the seaweed and the lobsters and boil for 8-10 minutes, just until lobsters are done. Reserve until service.

Briefly sauté the shallots in butter. Add the white wine and the vanilla bean. Reduce until almost dry. Add the cream and the fish glace. Reduce the heat and simmer about 5 minutes. At the last minute add the scallops just to warm. Correct the seasoning. Remove the pan from the heat and reserve, keeping warm.

Sauté the leek in the butter until tender but still green in color. Add the heavy cream. Season with salt and pepper and reduce to a low boil until the liquid almost evaporates and a thick sauce forms. Reserve, keeping warm.

Shell the lobster tails and claws. Slice the tails into medallions. On each serving plate, place one spoonful of the leeks and half a lobster. Spoon scallops on top of the leeks. Spoon the vanilla sauce over all. Garnish with the lobster heads, tails and legs. Yield: 4 servings.

From:

Froggy's
306 Green Bay Road
Highwood

68

Marinated Red Snapper with Sauce Nicoise

6 10-ounce portions of
red snapper, skinned

Marinade:
1 cup orange juice
½ cup soy sauce
½ teaspoon minced garlic
½ teaspoon Old Bay seasoning

Sauce Nicoise:
2 tablespoons marinade
¼ cup dry sherry
¼ cup white wine
3 tablespoons chicken stock
¼ cup finely chopped
green onions
1 tablespoon tuna, water pack
1 teaspoon tomato paste
1 teaspoon finely minced
black olives
¼ teaspoon minced garlic
½ cup heavy cream
5 egg yolks
12 ounces melted butter
4 teaspoons Grand Marnier or
4 teaspoons licorice flavored
liqueur

Combine the marinade ingredients; place fish in marinade and refrigerate at least 4 hours, preferably overnight.

Bring 2 tablespoons marinade, the sherry, the white wine, stock, onions and tuna to a boil, lower the heat and cook until the liquid is almost gone and the amount is reduced to 4 tablespoons.

Add the tomato paste, black olives, garlic and heavy cream, bring back to a boil and cook until thick and syrupy and mixture coats a spoon.

Place the egg yolks in a blender or food processor, with motor running add the butter in a slow, steady stream. Add the sauce mixture and blend till mixed. Add the liquor and blend again. Keep warm while preparing the fish.

Remove the fish from the marinade and pat dry. Brush fillets with melted butter and grill or broil until done. Place on warm serving plate and dress each piece with generous serving of the sauce. Yield: 6 servings.

From:

**The Mansion
at Golconda**
Columbus Street
Golconda

Poached Salmon with Dill Sauce

1 3-pound filet of salmon
3¼ cups water
2 teaspoons thyme
4 bay leaves
1 cup dry white wine or
    fish stock
1 teaspoon black pepper
1 cup chopped leaf celery
    or parsley

Dill sauce:
2 cups heavy cream
1 ounce shallots, chopped
1-1½ ounces chopped fresh dill
olive oil
1 cup fish stock
1 teaspoon fresh lemon juice
salt and white pepper to taste

Debone the salmon filet, remove the skin and cut into 8 6-ounce portions. Lay the portions of salmon in a heavy saucepan or poaching pan and cover with the water, thyme, bay leaves, white wine, pepper, and celery leaves.

Bring to a simmer over medium high heat. As soon as the stock starts to boil, reduce the heat and simmer over low heat for 10-15 minutes. Remove, keep fish warm, and reserve the stock.

For the sauce, reduce the cream by boiling, to one cup. Sauté the shallots and dill in a little olive oil, then add the stock and lemon juice. Bring to a boil over high heat and add the cream, mixing well. Serve the sauce over the fish and garnish with dill sprigs. A bottle of good dry white wine is recommended with the dish: a Sancerre, Pouilly Fume or Sylvaner Alsace. Yield: 8 servings.

From: **Cafe du Louvre**
               16 East Main Street
               Dundee

Salmon Framboise

4 6-ounce salmon filets
¾ cup clarified butter
⅓ cup raspberry vinegar
3 egg yolks
1 teaspoon water
salt and pepper to taste

Season the salmon filets and grill or sauté them in butter. In a small pan reduce the raspberry vinegar by ⅔. In the top of a double boiler combine the egg yolks and water, being careful not to let the boiling water touch the bottom of the top pan. Whip constantly until the mixture is hot, and thickened. Slowly pour in the butter and whip vigorously until the mixture has a mayonnaise appearance. Remove from the heat and add the reduced raspberry vinegar, while whipping constantly. Serve this raspberry hollandaise over the grilled salmon. Yield: 4 servings.

From:

**Le Radis Rouge/
Jumer's Chateau**
Jumer Drive
Bloomington

Grilled Alaskan King Salmon
with Ginger Lime Vinaigrette

8 8-ounce King Salmon steaks,
 1-inch thick
2 ounces olive oil

Ginger Lime Vinaigrette:
½ cup finely chopped fresh ginger
¼ cup finely chopped
 green onions
juice of 4 large limes
juice of 1 lemon*
3 kiwi fruit, peeled and chopped
1½ cups good olive oil

*enough juice to make ½ cup

When cutting the salmon steaks, it is best to cut them from one side of the salmon rather than cutting across the whole fish. If the steaks are too thick, butterfly them carefully. Use pliers to remove any pin bones. Brush the salmon steaks with the oil. Refrigerate.

Combine the above ingredients and whisk furiously. The sauce will be a light lime green with darker green flecks of onion and kiwi. Refrigerate for an hour or two to allow the flavors to meld. If you want the sauce more tart, add a little more lime or lemon juice. If too tart, add a little honey or sugar.

Build a fire on the grill. (I use pure hickory and oak charcoal, not briquettes.) Hold the steaks at room temperature about 20 minutes. Grill the steaks over medium-hot coals 3-4 minutes per side. Don't overcook!

Present the salmon napped over one corner with the vinaigrette. Garnish with fresh spinach leaves on one side and fresh asparagus or other fresh green vegetable on the other. Add wedges of lemon and lime and serve.

From: **Rick's,
An American Cafe**
Sunnycrest Mall #15
1717 Philo Road
Urbana

Salmon Grilled
with Red Onion Butter

2 6-ounce salmon filets
olive oil
salt and pepper to taste

Red Onion butter:
1 red onion, sliced
1 pound unsalted butter
pinch of salt
1 cup red wine
2 tablespoons cream

Garnish:
carrot curls
zucchini and squash slices
daikon slices*

*Japanese mild radish, available
in most produce sections.

Season filets. Brush with olive oil. Grill to medium.

For the butter, sweat the onions in a little butter with a pinch of salt, cover the pan and cook for 5 minutes. The moisture will be drawn out of the onions without caramelizing them. Add the red wine. Reduce, then add the cream, reduce until thick. Whip in the softened butter, one chunk at a time. Season with salt and pepper. Place salmon on plate; put the red onion butter on side. Garnish with fresh vegetables. Yield: 2 servings.

From: **Melange Restaurant**
1515 Sheridan, Plaza del Lago
Wilmette

Buttery Shrimp De Jonghe

⅔ cup butter
2 tablespoons dried chives
½ teaspoon garlic powder
⅛ teaspoon pepper
2 10-ounce packages
  frozen shrimp
1½ cups crushed bacon-flavored
  crackers

Preheat oven to 350 degrees. In a heavy, 2-quart saucepan melt the butter over medium heat. Add the chives, garlic powder and pepper, stir to blend. Dip the shrimp into this mixture and then roll in cracker crumbs to coat. Layer shrimp in an 8-inch square baking dish. Add rest of crumbs to remaining butter; stir to blend. Sprinkle shrimp with buttered crumbs. Bake in oven for 25-30 minutes or until shrimp are tender. Yield: 4 main course servings.

From: **The 518 South**
518 South State Street
Jerseyville

Shrimp in Dill Sauce

Some of the ingredients have no exact measurements. The reader will adjust the measurements to his or her own taste.

½ cup heavy cream
1 teaspoon fresh lemon juice
1 cup sliced mushrooms
white pepper to taste
1 tablespoon crème fraîche*
dried dill weed
2-3 tablespoons dry white wine
1 tablespoon unsalted butter
9 shelled shrimp, tail on
  for flavor
1 tablespoon each flour
  and butter

* To make crème fraîche take 1 pint of heavy cream and add either 1 or 2 teaspoons lemon juice, allowing the cream to stand out overnight.

In a sauté pan put all the ingredients together, stirring occasionally. As the sauce begins to bubble, check for consistency, adding small amounts of roux as needed. The sauce should be just thick enough to leave a clear trail behind a spoon when the spoon is run across the bottom of the pan. Too thick a sauce will taste of roux. Too thin and the sauce will taste of lemon and dill, and the presentation will not be as good.

When the shrimp are done and slightly red on the outside, turn off the heat, cover the pan and allow to sit for 2-3 minutes. Serve hot over rice with fresh lemon slices and sprigs of fresh dill.

From: **The Kingston Inn**
300 North Main Street
Galena

Walleye Pike Vidal

6 8-ounce filets of walleye pike
7-8 ounces clarified butter
¼ pound butter
6 ounces almonds
8-9 ounces seedless grapes
1 pound strawberries
4-5 ounces Amaretto
1 cup flour
salt and pepper to taste
2 16-inch skillets,
   preferably non-stick

Heat the clarified butter briefly in both skillets over high heat. Dredge pike filets in flour seasoned with salt and pepper, pat off excess and place in skillets, flesh side down. Sauté pike filets about 4 minutes, turn and sauté the other side for about 3 minutes. Cooking time will vary according to the thickness of the filets. Remove butter and add to one skillet the whole butter and almonds. Sauté, tossing often, until almonds are golden brown. Remove from heat and add Amaretto which will sizzle. Add the fruit and toss or stir so the Amaretto butter coats everything, but don't cook the fruit. Divide the mixture among 6 plates and serve with lemon and a green vegetable like broccoli. Garnish with a whole strawberry between broccoli and lemon.

From: **Rick's,
An American Cafe**
Sunnycrest Mall #15
1717 Philo Road
Urbana

FISH & SEAFOOD

Vegetables

Vegetables

Thank heavens the status of vegetables has changed and they have earned the respect of every-day cooks, as well as those who serve in restaurants. No longer are we subjected to objects thrown in a pot with the life boiled out of them until they're a gray and unidentifiable paste. No wonder children didn't like their vegetables!

Now we know how to cook vegetables properly to preserve color, texture, and nutrition. We are also doing imaginative things with them to add to their appeal and our repertoires as cooks. Here are some tasty dishes to try on your family.

Broccoli Mousseline

1 ounce butter
1 pound broccoli florets
¼ cup heavy cream
1 teaspoon salt
½ teaspoon white pepper
juice of ½ lemon
pinch nutmeg
4 eggs

Butter 6 individual ramekins, ½ cup each. Preheat oven to 375 degrees.

Wash the broccoli and cook in salted, boiling water until tender, approximately 10-12 minutes, then cool with ice immediately. Bring the heavy cream to a boil, add the broccoli, salt, white pepper, lemon juice and nutmeg. Cook until the cream is absorbed, about 8-10 minutes.

Puree the mixture in a food processor and add the eggs one at a time and blend well. Taste and correct seasoning. Fill the molds and cover each with a round of buttered foil.

Place in a water bath and put in the oven. Bake for 25 minutes or till firm. Yield: 6 servings.

From: **Le Radis Rouge/ Jumer's Chateau**
Jumer Road
Bloomington

Carrot Loaf

2 pounds of carrots,
  peeled and sliced
1 stick butter
¼ pound turnips,
  julienned
½ pound spinach,
  stems removed
5 eggs
4 ounces grated
  Swiss cheese
1 teaspoon salt
1 teaspoon pepper

Preheat oven to 350 degrees. Sauté the carrots in ½ stick of butter, until tender. Chop coarsely, set aside. Add more butter to the pan and sauté turnips till tender. Add to the carrots. Sauté spinach in the remaining butter. Chop coarsely and reserve separately. When spinach is cooled, add 1 egg. Beat remaining eggs and cheese together. Combine with the carrots and turnips. Add the salt and pepper.

Line a loaf pan with aluminum foil. Butter the foil. Fill the pan half full with carrot mixture, cover with spinach, top with remaining carrot mixture. Place in a pan of water, put the pan in the oven and bake for 1¼ hours or until a knife inserted in the center comes out clean. Invert onto platter and remove foil. Slice and serve. Yield: 6-8 servings.

From: **The Westerfield House**
Rural Route 2
Freeburg

Cauliflower in Curry and Mayonnaise

1-2 heads cauliflower,
  depending on size
½ tablespoon curry powder,
  your own blend, preferably
fresh sugar snap peas,
  julienned carrots for garnish

Mayonnaise:
2 whole eggs
dash salt
3-4 tablespoons fresh
  lemon juice
2 cups olive oil

Break the heads of cauliflowers into small florets and soak in cold water for at least 2 hours, then drain well.

Using a blender or food processor, blend together the eggs, salt and lemon juice. Blend only a few seconds. With the motor running add the olive oil in a thin stream. Be sure you add the oil slowly and steadily, this is the trick to successful mayonnaise. When all the oil is added and the mayonnaise is thickened, stop.

Put the well drained cauliflower in a large bowl and pour the mayonnaise over the top, blending in the curry powder as you stir in the mayonnaise. When you have achieved a consistent light yellow color, cover the bowl and place in the refrigerator for an hour or two to allow the flavors to blend.

Garnish with the fresh snap peas, julienned carrots or other colorful vegetables. Do not allow this dish to sit out on a warm day. Yield: 3-4 servings.

From: **The Kingston Inn**
300 North Main Street
Galena

French Green Beans Sauté

*20 ounces baby French
    green beans (haricots vert)
16 ounces small zucchini
14 ounces red bell pepper
3-4 ounces peanut oil
3 ounces chopped pecans
salt and pepper to taste*

Baby French green beans should be about 3-4 inches long. Trim the beans. Cut the zucchini the same length and roughly the same shape as the beans. Blanch the beans in a pot of simmering water and immediately refresh in cold water. Drain.

Simmer the whole red peppers in water for 2-3 minutes. Remove and grill over medium heat, turning constantly until skin is charred—or roast in a preheated 375 degree oven until charred, about 45 minutes. Gently remove the pepper skins with a paring knife. Remove the core and seeds, julienne the pepper. Careful—it will be quite soft, but sweet and smokey.

Sauté the beans and zucchini in the peanut oil for 3-4 minutes. Be careful not to crowd the pan too much. A wok works well for this dish. Toss the vegetables to stir them in the pan. After 2 minutes add the pecans. In the last 20 seconds add half the pepper. Salt and pepper to taste. Arrange the vegetables on the plates. Place the remaining pepper strips at right angles to the julienne, in stars—let your imagination be your guide. Heat the plates briefly in the oven and serve. Yield: 6 main servings or 10-12 side dishes.

From: **Rick's,
An American Cafe**
Sunnycrest Mall #15
1717 Philo Road
Urbana

Grilled Ratatouille

2½ pounds tomatoes,
  vine ripened
1½ pounds zucchini
12 ounces baby eggplant
2 ounces olive oil
1 small head radicchio
4 ounces spinach

Tomato Basil Sauce:
2 pounds tomatoes,
  peeled, seeded and chopped
2 tablespoons olive oil
2 garlic cloves, minced
3 ounces fresh basil leaves

Pesto:
1 cup fresh basil
2 large garlic cloves, minced
½ cup pine nuts
⅓-½ cup olive oil
freshly ground pepper to taste
½ cup freshly grated
  parmesan cheese

Slice the tomato, zucchini, and eggplant into rounds about ½-inch thick. Brush with olive oil. Prepare a fire and let burn down to coals until you have a medium fire. Grill the vegetable rounds carefully, not too many at once. The tomatoes will take about 2 minutes a side, the eggplant about 2½ minutes and the zucchini about 3 minutes. You will have to brush the eggplant and zucchini with more olive oil as it grills.

Remove and arrange on plate alternating colors. Dress the zucchini with the tomato-basil sauce and the eggplant with the pesto. Heat the plates in the oven briefly and garnish with leaves of radicchio and spinach. Cheese lovers may want to add some freshly grated parmesan before heating in the oven.

For the tomato basil sauce, cook the tomato in a skillet with the olive oil, garlic and basil. This is not a traditional tomato sauce so you should not cook it more than 4-5 minutes. The freshness of the ingredients should shine through.

In a food processor, combine the basil, garlic, pine nuts and process until well blended. Pour in the olive oil until the mixture resembles a light paste. Add freshly ground pepper to taste. Add the cheese and process briefly.

From: **Rick's,
An American Cafe**
Sunnycrest Mall #15
1717 Philo Road
Urbana

VEGETABLES

Salads &

Salad

Dressings

Salads & Salad Dressings

Salads and their dressings are one of the most versatile areas in which the cook can experiment. For the novice they resemble soups in that they are forgiving—with a little forethought most combinations will work.

This chapter contains some of Illinois chefs' and cooks' imaginative offerings, including a salad dressing that's been served in restaurants for close to fifty years. You can be sure that anything that's been served for that long and is still in demand, has to be worth trying.

Warm Goat Cheese Salad
with Wilted Red Onions
and Fresh Herbs

6 ounces goat cheese
olive oil
fresh tarragon, basil,
   chives or chervil
1 head Boston lettuce
1 head radicchio
4 ounces arugula
4 ounces mâche
½ head red leaf lettuce
¼ head curly endive
walnut oil to taste
sherry vinegar to taste
salt and pepper to taste
1 medium red onion, sliced
cracked black pepper
   and herbs

Slice the goat cheese into 4 portions; put into a glass dish. Add the olive oil and fresh herbs of your choice. Let marinate while preparing the rest of salad (up to 1 hour).

Rinse the greens and dry thoroughly. Toss the greens with walnut oil and sherry vinegar; season with salt, pepper and more herbs. Divide evenly among 4 plates.

Cook the red onion in some of the goat cheese marinade until wilted. Place over the tossed greens. In same pan, warm the goat cheese about 5 seconds on each side. Place on top of red onions and greens.

Pour extra walnut oil over the cheese; sprinkle with cracked black pepper and herbs. Yield: 4 servings.

From: **Melange Restaurant**
1515 Sheridan, Plaza del Lago
Wilmette

Red and Green Salad
with Grilled Chicken and Goat Cheese

12 ounces goat cheese
1 ounce fresh basil leaves,
   chopped
4 ounces olive oil
1 head radicchio
1 head red leaf lettuce
1 head Bibb lettuce
1 head purple flowering kale
1 bunch (10 ounces) spinach
24 ounces boneless chicken
   breasts, skinless
16 cherry tomatoes

Raspberry Sauce:
2 10-ounce packages frozen
   raspberries, thawed
3 tablespoons lemon juice
3 tablespoons sugar
1 ounce port

Raspberry Vinaigrette:
10 ounces raspberry sauce
1 ounce balsamic vinegar
3 ounces red wine vinegar
5 ounces olive oil
2 ounces walnut oil

For the salad, carefully cut the goat cheese into 8 rounds. Make a marinade by placing the basil leaves in the olive oil. Place the goat cheese rounds in the marinade and put in a cool place for 2-3 hours.

Trim the stems, cores and so on from the radicchio, lettuces, kale and spinach. Rinse and dry them. Tear them into large bite-size pieces, place in a bowl and refrigerate.

Grill the chicken over medium hot coals. Let rest at room temperature for 10 minutes and then make thin slices on the bias.

Toss the salad with 16-20 ounces of the raspberry vinaigrette. Arrange on 8 plates. Arrange the chicken and cherry tomatoes over the salad. Place a goat cheese round in the center of each plate. Dot the chicken and cheese with the raspberry vinaigrette. Yield: 8 servings.

For the sauce, simmer the berries in a little water for 5 minutes. Force through a sieve to remove the seeds. Add the other ingredients and simmer for 3 minutes. Add a little cornstarch, if necessary, to thicken the sauce.

For the vinaigrette, whisk all the ingredients furiously in a bowl. This vinaigrette is heavily weighted toward the fruity, raspberry flavor, hence the unusual proportion of oil to vinegar.

From: **Rick's,
An American Cafe**
Sunnycrest Mall #15
1717 Philo Road
Urbana

Sweet Lemon Dressing

4 egg yolks
½ cup sugar
⅓ cup fresh lemon juice
¾ cup salad oil
½ cup heavy cream, whipped

Combine the egg yolks, sugar and lemon juice in the blender or electric mixer. Whip until frothy and light yellow.

Add oil slowly, whisking in so the oil is thoroughly blended.

Add in the whipped cream. Keep chilled.

From: **The Eagle Ridge Inn & Resort**
Highway 20 East
Galena

Aunt May's Salad Dressing

This recipe is the most often requested at Silver Annie's and was the invention of Aunt May, who was a restaurant cook for thirty-one years!

 2 eggs, lightly beaten
½ teaspoon salt
dash paprika
dash black pepper
¼ teaspoon garlic salt
1 cup olive oil
1 cup white vinegar
1 green pepper
1 pimento
½ cup sugar

Begin by lightly beating eggs. Add in the salt, paprika, pepper and garlic salt, whisking continously.

Continuing to whisk slowly, add in the olive oil and vinegar. Chop the green pepper and pimento very fine and add to the mixture.

Then add the sugar, tasting to be sure it doesn't get too sweet. More sugar may be added to taste. Refrigerate. Yield: approximately 1 pint of dressing.

From: **Silver Annie's**
124 North Commerce Street
Galena

Poppy Seed Salad Dressing

1½ cups sugar
1¾ teaspoons ground mustard
1¾ teaspoons salt
⅔ cup red wine vinegar
2 tablespoons chopped onion
1½ teaspoons poppy seeds
2 cups salad oil

Put the sugar, mustard and salt in a non-reactive pan. Mix well. Add the vinegar. Whip with wire whisk. Heat to lukewarm. Add the onion and poppyseeds. Gradually add in the oil, continuing to whisk until all the oil has been added. If oil is not added gradually, the dressing will separate and not thicken. This dressing is excellent over fruit salad or any salad where a sweet-sour dressing is appropriate. Yield: 3 cups.

From: **The 518 Restaurant**
518 South State Street
Jerseyville

92

SALADS & SALAD DRESSINGS

Desserts

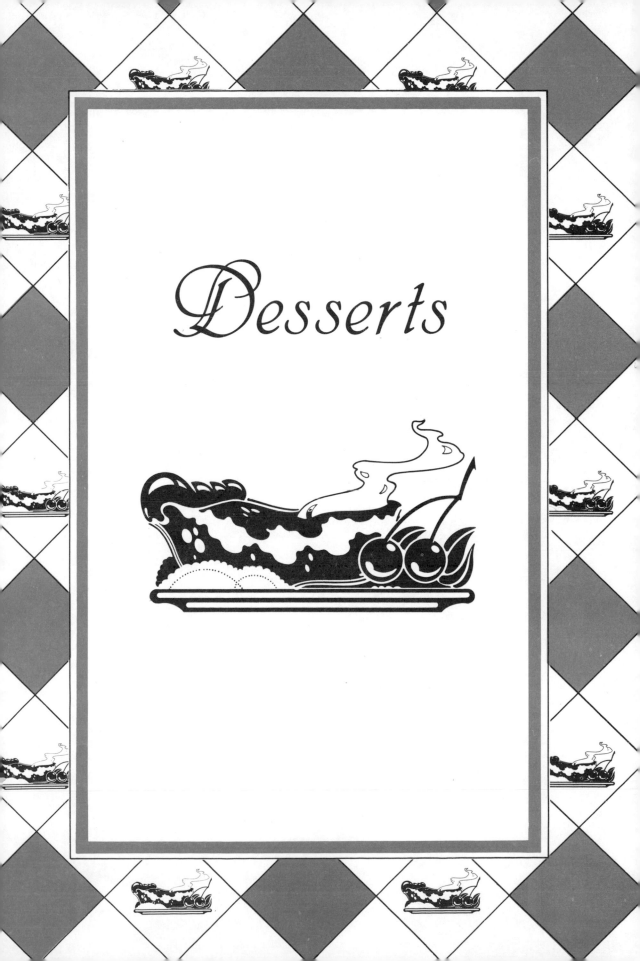

Desserts

Just the word dessert alerts the diner to good things ahead. All of us have our own expectations of dessert, whether from early bribery to eat our broccoli or spinach to memories of Mom's apple pie or an adult and unshakable addiction to dark chocolate.

I think you'll agree that Illinois chefs have created something for every palate. Lots to do with strawberries, three cheesecakes—classic, Chocolate Mocha and Strawberry. There's a diet buster named for Illinois' present governor, Jim Thompson. A classic French recipe for Cherries Clafoutis, a Black Forest Torte—if you can't find something tempting here, maybe you should re-examine your attitude towards dessert.

Alpine White Chocolate Mousse Cake

Cake:
12 ounces white chocolate,
  divided
½ cup shortening
2 cups flour
1½ cups sugar
4 teaspoons baking powder
1 teaspoon salt
1 cup milk
1 teaspoon vanilla
4 egg whites (½ cup)
⅔ pecan pieces

Frosting:
3 ounces white chocolate,
  melted and cooled
2 cups heavy cream
pecan halves

Preheat the oven to 350 degrees. Grease and flour two 8-inch round cake pans. Melt 2 ounces of the white chocolate in a small bowl with the shortening, set aside.

Measure flour, sugar, baking powder and salt into a bowl. Add the shortening/chocolate mixture, ⅔ cup of milk and the vanilla, blend 1 minute on low speed of electric mixer. Beat 2 minutes at high speed, scraping sides of bowl occasionally. Add the remaining milk and the egg whites, beat 2 minutes on high speed, scraping the bowl occasionally. Pour into prepared pans and top cake batter with ⅓ cup of white chocolate chips or small chunks and ⅔ cup pecan pieces. Bake 30-35 minutes or until toothpick inserted in the center comes out clean. Cool. Remove from pans.

Whip the cream to soft peaks. Add the cooled, melted white chocolate and whip, scraping the sides of the bowl. Frost the top and sides of the cake, with chip and nut layer facing upward. Decorate with swirls of whipped cream and pecan halves.

From: **Rockford Woman's Club Food Shop**
405 North Church Street
Rockford

Baked Alaska
"Close Encounter"

2 9-inch genoise layers
$\frac{1}{3}$ gallon chocolate mousse
   ice cream
$\frac{1}{3}$ gallon French vanilla
   ice cream
3 ounces Frangelico liquer
15 egg whites, save shells
1 teaspoon cream of tartar
4 tablespoons sugar
3-4 ounces brandy
1 ovenproof platter with
   raised edge

Cut each genoise in half horizontally to make 4 rounds. Trim 1 round to 6-inch diameter. Place that on platter.

Alternately layer chocolate and vanilla ice cream to form mountain. Cut the remaining cake into 1 x 2-inch rectangles and 1 x 2½ x 2½-inch triangles (10 of each) and completely cover the ice cream with them. Lace the cake thoroughly with the Frangelico. Wrap and freeze for 2-3 hours.

Twenty minutes before serving, whip the egg whites, which should be room temperature, until they form medium stiff peaks—halfway through, add the sugar.

Preheat the oven to 450 degrees. Remove the Alaska from the freezer and cover it with the egg whites to make a volcano. Do it with a flourish, forming peaks, valleys, ridges, etc.

Take a large ½ eggshell and cut ridges into it, giving it a jagged edge. Place in the meringue at the top of the mountain to form a cone. Fill the shell with brandy. Bake in the preheated oven for 3-4 minutes until the meringue is golden brown.

Dim the lights in the dining room, carefully ignite the remaining brandy in a small saucepan and spoon the flaming brandy into the brandy-filled shell. You'll create a flaming peak with dramatic lava flow down the mountain. Serve immediately. Yield: 1 spectacular baked Alaska.

From: **Rick's,**
                An American Cafe
                     Sunnycrest Mall #15
                        1717 Philo Road
                              Urbana

Banana Fudge Walnut Cake

2 layers good devil's food cake*
8 bananas
½ teaspoon cinnamon
2-3 tablespoons gelatin
½ cup water
1 cup simple syrup**
1½ cups walnuts, ground
2 cups heavy cream
2 teaspoons vanilla
¼ cup powdered sugar

*"The Joy of Cooking" has a good basic devil's food cake recipe.

**Simple syrup is simply sugar and water brought to boil so the sugar is completely dissolved.

Puree 5 of the bananas. Add cinnamon and 1 cup of the walnuts. Dissolve the gelatin in the water. Heat the banana mixture, add the dissolved gelatin and stir until smooth.

Cut each cake layer in half horizontally.

Pour simple syrup over each layer of cake. Put one layer of cake on plate, top with banana puree and a layer of banana slices. Add the second cake layer and repeat the process until all the cake layers and bananas have been used. Beat the whipping cream with the vanilla; when soft peaks have formed add the sugar a little at a time and continue beating until stiff peaks form. Frost the cake with the whipped cream, sprinkle remaining walnuts on top of cake and serve. Yield: 1 cake.

From: **Rick's, An American Cafe**
Sunnycrest Mall #15
1717 Philo Road
Urbana

Biscuit Sabayon
of Coconut, Pineapple and Rum Sauce

Biscuits:
2 cups flour
½ cup ground almonds
1 cup shredded, unsweetened coconut
½ teaspoon salt
2 sticks unsalted butter
½ cup water

Pineapple Cream:
3 cups heavy cream
¼ cup powdered sugar
½ cup puree of fresh pineapple

Rum Sauce:
4 egg yolks
½ cup sugar
1 teaspoon cornstarch
1¾ cups boiling milk
¼-½ cups dark rum

Preheat oven to 350 degrees. For the biscuits, combine the flour, almonds, coconut and salt in a food processor. Add the butter and pulse chop until incorporated. With the processor running, add the water a tablespoonful at a time until mixture lightly clings together.

Form into ball, wrap in wax paper and refrigerate for 1 hour. Roll out between sheets of wax paper to ¼-inch thickness and cut into 4-inch rounds. Bake in the oven for 4-6 minutes, till lightly browned. Set aside.

For the pineapple cream, whip the heavy cream until thick, fold in the sugar and the pineapple. Set aside.

In the mixer beat the egg yolks with the sugar and cornstarch. Bring the milk to a boil and add to the mixture. Place mixture in a heavy bottomed saucepan and cook over low heat until it begins to thicken. Immediately remove from the heat and place in a cool container. Add the rum and set aside.

To assemble pipe the pineapple cream between two biscuits and surround with the rum sauce. Garnish the top with toasted coconut and place small pineapple slices around each biscuit. Yield: 6 servings.

From: **Tallgrass Restaurant**
1006 South State Street
Lockport

Black Forest Torte

6 eggs
1 cup sugar
½ cup + 3 tablespoons cake flour
4 tablespoons cornstarch
6 tablespoons cocoa
3 tablespoons melted butter

Preheat the oven to 375 degrees. Butter and flour a 10-inch springform pan. Combine the eggs and sugar and warm over warm water to about 95 degrees, stirring constantly. Beat to a heavy sponge with electric mixer. When mixture is stiff enough to hold shape momentarily when cut through, fold in the cake flour. To measure the cake flour, sift the flour into the measures. Then sift the cake flour together with the cornstarch and unsweetened cocoa. Fold the sifted mixture into the eggs and sugar mixture. Then fold in the melted butter.

Bake at 375 degrees for 20-25 minutes or until a toothpick inserted in the center comes out clean. Cool on a wire rack and then refrigerate.

½ cup sugar
1 cup water
1 orange wedge with skin
1 lemon wedge with skin

1 can dark sweet cherries
1 can sour pie cherries
½ cup kirschwasser brandy

4 cups heavy cream
3 tablespoons powdered sugar
1 teaspoon vanilla
3 ounces bittersweet chocolate, melted

Bring to a boil the sugar, water, orange and lemon wedge. Simmer for 3-4 minutes. Discard citrus, cool.

Drain and discard the juice of the canned cherries.

With a serrated knife cut the cake horizontally into 3 layers. Soak each layer in a combination of syrup and the kirschwasser, using a pastry brush to apply.

Whip the cream, sugar and vanilla to stiff peaks. Add the melted chocolate to 2 cups of the whipped cream, adding in the remaining syrup.

Place one layer of the cake soaked in kirschwasser syrup on a plate, top with all of the chocolate whipped cream. On top place all but 13 of the dark sweet cherries.

Add the second layer of cake. Top with more of the whipped cream and the sour cherries. Add the last layer of cake, covering cake with the remaining whipped cream, reserving enough for 13 rosettes. Shave dark, sweet chocolate over the entire top of the cake. Pipe 13 rosettes on the top around the edges. Place 13 black cherries in the rosettes. Refrigerate at least 3 hours before serving.

From: **The Intermezzo Cafe**
The Krannert Center
for the Performing Arts
Urbana

Carrot Cake

Cake:
2 cups sugar
2 cups flour
3 cups grated carrot
1½ cups oil
4 eggs
2 teaspoons baking soda
2 teaspoons baking powder
2 teaspoons cinnamon
1 cup pecan pieces

Frosting:
8 ounces cream cheese
1 pound powdered sugar
1 stick margarine
1 teaspoon vanilla

Grease and flour an 11 x 13-inch cake pan. Preheat the oven to 350 degrees.

Place all the ingredients for the cake in the large bowl of a mixer. Mix until thoroughly combined. Pour into the prepared pan. Bake approximately 55 minutes or until a toothpick inserted in the middle comes out clean. Let cool completely.

Mix the frosting ingredients until smooth. Frost the cooled cake. Yield: 12-16 servings.

From:

**Cindi's Cafe
& Catering**
222 South 9th Street
Mt. Vernon

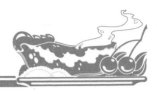

Hawaiian Carrot Cake

2 cups sugar
1½ cups vegetable oil
3 eggs
2 teaspoons vanilla
2¼ cups flour
1½ teaspoons cinnamon
2 teaspoons baking soda
1 teaspoon salt
2 cups grated carrots
1 cup crushed pineapple, drained
1 cup raisins
2 cups coconut
1 cup chopped walnuts

Frosting:
3 ounces cream cheese
4 tablespoons melted butter
2 tablespoons milk
1 teaspoon vanilla
⅛ teaspoon salt
3½ cups powdered sugar

Preheat oven to 350 degrees. Grease a 9½ x 13-inch pan.

Combine the sugar, oil, eggs and vanilla in a large bowl. Mix well.

Sift together the flour, cinnamon, baking soda, and salt. Stir in the egg mixture. Mix well.

Fold in the carrots, drained pineapple, raisins, coconut, and walnuts. Pour into pan and bake 40-45 minutes or until a toothpick inserted in the center comes out clean. Cool completely.

For the frosting combine the cream cheese, butter, milk, vanilla and salt. Beat well. Beat in enough sugar to make a spreadable consistency. Spread on cool cake. Yield: 12 servings.

From: **Elsah's Landing Restaurant**
18 La Salle Street
Elsah

Carrot, Zucchini, Parsnip Cake

3 cups flour
3 cups sugar
1 teaspoon salt
1 tablespoon baking soda
1 tablespoon cinnamon
1½ cups corn oil
4 eggs
1 teaspoon vanillla
1½ cups chopped walnuts
1 cup shredded coconut
1 cup grated carrots
½ cup grated zucchini
½ cup grated parsnip
¾ cup drained crushed pineapple

Frosting:
8 ounces cream cheese
2 ounces softened unsalted butter
1½ cups powdered sugar

Preheat oven to 350 degrees. Grease and flour 2 9-inch cake pans.

Sift all the dry ingredients for the cake together. In the large bowl of a mixer, blend the oil, eggs and vanilla. Mix in the dry ingredients, blending thoroughly. Add the remaining ingredients and blend thoroughly. Place in the prepared cake pans and bake for approximately 30 minutes or until a toothpick inserted in the center comes out clean. Cool cakes completely.

Cream the cheese and butter, gradually adding the sifted sugar until a spreadable consistency has been reached. Assemble and frost the cakes. Refrigerate until ready to serve. Yield: 10-12 servings.

From: **The Public Landing**
200 West 8th Street
Lockport

Strawberry Layer Cake

Cake:
6 eggs, separated
1 teaspoon vanilla
1 teaspoon grated lemon rind
1 cup sugar
1 cup flour
½ cup butter, melted

2 pints fresh strawberries, sliced

Frosting:
6 egg yolks
1 cup sugar
½ cup water
1½ cups unsalted butter,
   whipped
½ cup strawberry puree
red food color

Preheat the oven to 350 degrees. Butter and line 3 9-inch cake pans. Beat the egg yolks with vanilla and lemon rind until yolks are pale and 3 times in volume.

Beat the whites until soft peaks form. Gradually, add the sugar a tablespoon at a time, beating until stiff peaks form.

Pour yolks over whites and gently fold together. Sift flour over the eggs and fold gently. Fold in melted butter. Pour into cake pans and bake for 15-20 minutes. Cake should spring back when touched gently. Let cool 4 minutes. Then invert onto rack and cool completely.

Beat the egg yolks until tripled in volume. Meanwhile combine the sugar and water in a saucepan and heat until it comes to a boil. Let it boil until it reaches the soft ball stage on the candy thermometer.

Carefully pour the sugar syrup directly into the yolk, while still beating. Be careful as it may splatter. Continue beating until bowl is lukewarm to the touch. Add the whipped and softened butter by the tablespoon. Frosting should be thick and mound on itself. Add the strawberry puree and enough food coloring to make frosting a light pink color.

Using a serrated knife, split each cake layer in half horizontally. Place one bottom half of cake on platter and spread enough frosting to cover layer. Spread ⅕ sliced strawberries over frosting. Place top half of layer over strawberries. Layering cake, strawberries and frosting until the top of the last layer. Let set in cool place before frosting the outside and top of the cake. Refrigerate overnight or several hours before serving. Before slicing to serve, let stand at room temperature for 20-30 minutes.

From:

Rick's,
An American Cafe
Sunnycrest Mall #15
1717 Philo Road
Urbana

Cheesecake Kingston Inn

Pie crust—graham cracker,
ground nut or other of your
choice
1 tablespoon unflavored gelatin
½ cup water
2 egg yolks
⅓ cup sugar
8 ounces cream cheese
⅓ cup sour cream
¾ cup heavy cream
apricot preserves, (optional)

Dissolve the unflavored gelatin in the water over a bain-marie or double boiler so that gelatin won't lump.

Beat the egg yolks, adding the sugar, mixing well. While still mixing, add room temperature cream cheese. When mixed well, add the sour cream. Slowly add the heavy cream, continuing to mix until very light and fluffy. Adjust the mixer to a slow speed, adding the gelatin mixture. Be sure the gelatin is not too hot to the touch or it may lump in the mixture.

When the gelatin is well mixed, allow the mixture to set for a time. Pour into the pie crust, which you may line with apricot preserves, if so desired. Almost any kind of preserves may be used, but apricot seems to taste best.

From: **The Kingston Inn**
300 North Main Street
Galena

Chocolate Mocha Cheesecake

Crust:
1½ cups chocolate wafer crumbs
1 cup blanched almonds, toasted
  and chopped
⅓ cup sugar
½ teaspoon espresso powder
6 tablespoons butter, softened

Filling:
1½ pounds cream cheese,
  softened
1 cup sugar
4 eggs
⅓ cup heavy cream
¼ cup Tia Maria
5 tablespoons instant
  decaffeinated coffee
1 teaspoon vanilla

Topping:
1 cup sour cream
1 tablespoon sugar
1 teaspoon vanilla
grated chocolate

For the crust, preheat oven to 375 degrees. Butter a 9½-inch springform pan.

In a bowl combine the wafer crumbs, the almonds, sugar, espresso powder and butter. Mix well and pat onto the bottom and sides of the springform pan.

For the filling, in a large bowl cream together the softened cream cheese, the sugar and the eggs, beating in one at a time and beating well after each addition. Add the heavy cream and the Tia Maria in which you have dissolved the instant coffee. Add the vanilla and beat until light. Pour batter into the prepared shell and bake for 30 minutes. Transfer the cake to a rack to cool.

In a bowl combine the sour cream, sugar and vanilla, spread the mixture evenly on the cake and bake for 5 minutes more. Transfer the cake to the rack, let cool completely, then chill, lightly covered overnight. Remove the sides of the pan, transfer the cake to a plate and top with grated chocolate.

From: **Rockford Woman's
          Club Food Shop**
          405 North Church Street
          Rockford

Strawberry Cheesecake

1 pound ricotta cheese
1 pound sour cream
1 pound cream cheese
1½ cups sugar
4 ounces melted butter
3 eggs
3 tablespoons flour
3 tablespoons cornstarch
4½ teaspoons vanilla
1 cup strawberry puree

Preheat oven to 375 degrees. Grease and flour a 10-inch springform pan. Wrap foil around the pan to prevent leakage.

Combine the first three ingredients in a bowl and beat until fluffy. Add the rest of the ingredients, except the strawberry puree, and beat on high speed until smooth, about 9-10 minutes. Fold in the strawberry puree.

Pour into the pan and bake for 1 hour. Turn the oven off and leave the cake in the oven for an additional hour. Refrigerate several hours or overnight before serving.

From: **Rick's
An American Cafe**
Sunnycrest Mall #15
1717 Philo Road
Urbana

Cherry Clafoutis

1 pound fresh cherries, pitted
½ cup kirsch
1 tablespoon sugar

Pastry:
1 cup flour
2 tablespoons sugar
¼ teaspoon salt
6 tablespoons unsalted butter
1 egg yolk
½ teaspoon vanilla
1 tablespoon fresh lemon juice

Filling:
4 eggs
1 cup heavy cream
½ cup sugar
1 teaspoon vanilla
2 tablespoons cake flour
2 tablespoons kirsch

Put cherries into a large bowl. Add the kirsch and sugar. Let marinate for 2 hours, stirring occasionally.

For the pastry, mix flour, 2 tablespoons sugar and salt in a large bowl. Cut in butter until mixture resembles coarse crumbs. Make a well in the center of the flour, add the egg yolk, vanilla and lemon juice. Mix with a fork just until dough gathers into a ball. Wrap and refrigerate for 30 minutes.

Preheat oven to 325 degrees. Roll out the dough on a lightly floured surface. Fit into a 10-inch tart pan with removable bottom. Refrigerate for 5 minutes.

For the filling, mix the eggs, cream, sugar, vanilla, flour and kirsch together. Drain cherries, remove the pan with dough from the refrigerator. Arrange cherries carefully in the tart pan. Carefully pour the egg cream mixture over the cherries.

Bake for 40-45 minutes until knife inserted 1 inch from edge and withdrawn is clean. Do not overbake. Cool on wire rack, serve warm. Yield: 8 servings.

From: **Le Francais**
269 South Milwaukee Street
Wheeling

Chocolate Pâté

1 pound bittersweet chocolate
1 cup heavy cream
4 tablespoons melted butter
4 egg yolks, beaten
¼ cup dark rum,
    Grand Marnier, or Frangelico
8 ounces pistachios,
    or cashews, chopped

Line a small bread pan with plastic wrap. Melt the chocolate in a double boiler or bain-marie.

Combine the chocolate, cream, butter, beaten egg yolks and liquor. Mix thoroughly. Put ½ of the mixture in the loaf pan, thump on the counter to settle. Sprinkle with the nuts, add the rest of the chocolate.

Cover and put in freezer for 3-4 hours. Unmold by dipping the pan in hot water for a few seconds. Slice and serve with zabaglione or raspberry sauce given in recipe for baked brie. Yield: 6-8 servings.

From: **Eagle Ridge Inn & Resort**
Highway 20 East
Galena

Ambrosia Pie

10-inch pie crust,
  baked and cooled

Filling:

⅔ cup sugar
⅓ cup flour
1 cup milk
1 cup orange juice
2 tablespoons lemon juice
2 tablespoons orange zest,
  divided
5 eggs, separated
1 cup coconut, divided
½ cup sliced almonds
½ teaspoon cornstarch
⅓ cup sugar
½ teaspoon cream of tartar

In an ovenproof mixing bowl, combine the flour and sugar; whisk in milk, then whisk in orange juice. Add the lemon juice and one tablespoon of the orange zest. Microwave on high power in 3 minute stages, whisking until smooth and thickened. Whisk some of the hot custard into 5 egg yolks, then blend together. Microwave 2 more minutes, blend until smooth, and add coconut, reserving 2 tablespoonsful for garnish. Add the almonds. Cool in refrigerator or pan of ice water to lukewarm.

Preheat oven to 375 degrees. Prepare meringue using egg whites with the cornstarch and cream of tartar. Add the sugar a tablespoon at a time once soft peaks have formed, until all the sugar has been incorporated and the meringue holds stiff peaks.

Pour the custard filling into the baked pie shell; pile meringue topping over the custard, spreading to the edges and sealing the custard. Garnish with the reserved orange zest and coconut. Bake in the oven for 10-15 minutes until nicely browned on top. Yield: 1 10-inch pie.

From: **The Mansion at
Golconda**
Columbus Street
Golconda

French Silk Pie

1 pie crust, baked and cooled
    graham cracker or your
    preference

3½ sticks unsalted butter
2 eggs, chilled
¾ cup sugar
1 teaspoon vanilla
½ cup chocolate syrup

Soften the butter to room temperature. Crack the eggs open while still cold. Put the butter, eggs, sugar, vanilla and chocolate into a mixing bowl and at moderate speed, blend all ingredients. Watch and listen for a change in consistency. The pie filling will thicken and the mixer will make a different sound.

When this occurs, usually after about 10 minutes or slightly less, pour the mixture into the pie crust. Allow the pie several hours in the refrigerator to set up. Be sure to cover the pie as it will absorb ordors from other foods. Yield: 1 pie.

From: **The Kingston Inn**
300 North Main Street
Galena

The Jim Thompson Diet Buster Pie

1 10-inch pie shell, unbaked
½ cup coconut
½ cup shelled pistachios
½ cup mini chocolate chips
½ cup butterscotch sauce
3 eggs
1½ cups sugar
½ cup flour
2 tablespoons cognac
1 cup mini chocolate chips
¼ cup butter

Preheat oven to 450 degrees. Mix together the coconut, pistachios, ½ cup chocolate chips, and the butterscotch sauce/ice cream topping. Spread in the bottom of the pie crust.

Whisk the eggs till blended. Add the sugar and blend. Add flour and blend again. Add the cognac and whip until smooth. Melt the chocolate chips and butter over boiling water and add to the filling. Pour filling mixture over the butterscotch mixture and bake for 10 minutes at 450 degrees. Lower the temperature to 350 degrees and bake 30-40 minutes or until filling is set and crust is lightly browned. Cool completely before cutting and serving. May be accompanied by unsweetened whipped cream.

From:

The Mansion at Golconda
Columbus Street
Golconda

Peanut Butterscotch Pie

1 10-inch unbaked pie shell

4 eggs
½ cup brown sugar
1 cup white corn syrup
¼ cup melted butter
⅓ cup butterscotch liqueur
1 cup salted chopped peanuts
½ cup peanut butter

Preheat oven to 450 degrees. Whisk eggs until smooth. Add the sugar, corn syrup, butter and liqueur and whisk until smooth. Add the nuts. Spread the peanut butter in the bottom of the pie shell. Gently pour in the filling. Bake 10 minutes at 450 degrees; reduce the heat to 350 degrees and bake 30-40 minutes until set.

From:

The Mansion at Golconda
Columbus Street
Golconda

Raspberry Satin Pie

Pie crust of your choice, if regular
   pastry, should be baked first
3½ sticks unsalted butter
2 eggs, chilled
¾ cup sugar
1 teaspoon vanilla
2 tablespoons creme de cassis
1 cup pureed and strained
   raspberries

Soften the butter to room temperature. Crack the eggs open while still chilled. Add butter, eggs, sugar, vanilla, creme de cassis, and the pureed raspberries together in a large mixing bowl. Blend carefully at moderate speed. Watch and listen for a change in consistency. The pie filling will thicken and the mixer sound will be different.

When this occurs, after close to 10 minutes, pour mixture, scraping with a soft spatula, into the pie crust. Allow several hours in the refrigerator for the pie to set up and form. Be sure to cover since the filling will absorb odors from other food.

From: **The Kingston Inn**
300 North Main Street
Galena

Strawberry Rhubarb Pie

Pie crust:
2 cups flour
1 teaspoon salt
½ teaspoon cream of tartar
2 tablespoons sugar
⅔ cup shortening
⅓ cup cold water

Filling:
2½ cups thickly sliced rhubarb
½ cup sugar
5 tablespoons cornstarch
1 teaspoon salt
2½ cups strawberries

For the pie crust, sift the dry ingredients together. Cut the shortening into the dry ingredients with a pastry blender until it resembles coarse meal. Using a large fork, blend the water into the mixture. The mixture should form a ball and pull away from the sides of the bowl.

Roll half the dough out onto a floured surface, using a floured rolling pin. Line a 9-inch pie pan with the dough.

Preheat the oven to 350 degrees. Put the rhubarb in a bowl with the sugar, cornstarch and salt. Mix together and let sit for 5 minutes. Mix in the strawberries, which you have cut in half. Pour into the pie shell.

Roll out dough for the top crust. Place dough on top of pie and crimp edges together. Make steam slits in top crust. Brush with an egg wash made with 1 egg beaten in a little cold water. Sprinkle with sugar. Bake for 45 minutes or until crust is light brown. Let cool slightly before serving. Yield: 1 9-inch pie.

From:
**Rick's,
An American Cafe**
Sunnycrest Mall #15
1717 Philo Road
Urbana

Viennese Fresh Fruit Tart

1 pie shell, baked in a tart pan
   with a removable bottom
1 layer genoise*
1 recipe Bavarian cream
1 jar apricot jam
½ cup rum
½-1 cup heavy cream
kiwi fruit
strawberries
peaches
raspberries
grapes, seedless
nectarines
apricots

Recipes for Bavarian cream and genoise can be found in "Mastering the Art of French Cooking," by Simone Beck, Julia Child and Louise Bertholle.

On a serving plate place the baked pie shell, add 1-2 cups of the Bavarian cream depending on the size and depth of the pie shell. Put the cake layer, which should be no more than ½-inch thick, on top of the custard. Sprinkle the cake with the rum.

Peel and cut the fruit, using at least 3 kinds selected for contrast in color, texture and flavor. Arrange attractively on the cake in a circular pattern.

While you're doing this, warm the apricot jam until it is liquid but not hot. You may need to add a couple of tablespoons of water if the jam is too thick for a good spreading consistency.

Brush the jam onto the fruit, totally covering it so the air will not get to the fresh fruit and darken it.

Whip cream and pipe on tart around edges, leaving fruit exposed in center.

From: **The Intermezzo Cafe**
Krannert Center for
the Performing Arts
Urbana

Inns & Restaurants

The numbers in parentheses after the name of the restaurant refer to the pages on which recipes from each establishment appear.

Le Titi de Paris
1015 West Dundee Road
Arlington Heights
312/506-0222
Reservations suggested
Luncheon Tuesday-Friday
Dinner Tuesday-Saturday
Credit cards: V, MC, AE, DC, CB
(49, 59)

Central Station Cafe
220 East Front Street
Bloomington
309/828-2323
Reservations accepted
Credit cards: V, MC
(14, 36)

Le Radis Rouge/Jumer's Chateau
Jumer Drive
Bloomington
309/638-1133
Reservations requested
Credit cards: V, MC, AE
(38, 58, 70, 79)

The North End Market Restaurant
395 North Kinzie Street
Bradley
815/933-7900
Reservations accepted
Credit cards: V, MC
(3, 4)

The Autumn Tree
201 West Springfield Avenue
Champaign
217/359-0699
Reservations recommended
Credit cards: V, MC
(24, 26)

Eberhard's
117 North Main Street
Columbia
618/281-5400
Reservations advised
Credit cards: V, MC, AE, DC, CB
(4)

Nick's Cafe
480 Brush College Road
Decatur
217/422-2255
No reservations
No credit cards
(8)

Sayat Nova
20 West Golf Road
Des Plaines
312/296-1776
Reservations accepted
Credit cards: V, MC, AE, DC
(50)

Cafe de Louvre
16 East Main Street
East Dundee
312/428-8000
Reservations advised
Credit cards: V, MC
(35, 57, 69)

Chez Seamus French Cafe
The Village at Ginger Creek, #10
Edwardsville
618/656-7395
Reservations advised
Credit cards: V, MC
(7, 28)

Elsah's Landing Restaurant
18 La Salle Street
Elsah
618/374-1607
Reservations for luncheon
    and tea only
No credit cards
(13, 33, 34, 41, 101)

The Westerfield House
Rural Route 2
Freeburg
618/539-5643
Reservations required
Credit cards: V, MC, AE
(16, 17, 23, 80)

Eagle Ridge Inn & Resort
Highway 20 East
Galena
815/777-2444
Reservations recommended
Credit cards: V, MC
(21, 40, 54, 65, 89, 108)

Farmers' Home Hotel
334 Spring Street
Galena
815/777-3456
Reservations recommended
Credit cards: V, MC
(5)

The Kingston Inn
300 North Main Street
Galena
815/777-0451
Reservations suggested
Credit cards: V, MC, AE
(27, 45, 63, 66, 74, 81, 104, 110, 113)

Silver Annie's
124 North Commerce Street
Galena
815/777-3131
Reservations accepted
Credit cards: V, MC
(90)

The Mansion at Golconda
Columbus Avenue
Golconda
618/683-4400
Reservations necessary
Credit cards: V, MC, AE
(42, 56, 64, 68, 109, 111, 112)

Froggy's
306 North Green Bay Street
Highwood
312/433-7080
Reservations accepted
Credit cards: V, MC, DC
(66)

The 518 South
518 South State Street
Jerseyville
618/498-4011
Reservations preferred
Credit cards: V, MC, AE
(73, 91)

Tallgrass Restaurant
1006 South State Street
Lockport
815/838-5566
Reservations mandatory
Credit cards: V, MC
(28, 53, 98)

The Public Landing Restaurant
200 West 8th Street
Lockport
815/838-6500
Reservations for large groups
No credit cards
(6, 22, 51, 102)

The Rockwell Inn
2400 West Route 6
Morris
815/942-6224
Reservations accepted,
    required on weekends
Credit cards: V, MC, AE, DC, CB
(48)

Cindi's Cafe & Catering
222 South 9th Street
Mount Vernon
618/242-6221
No reservations
No credit cards
(39, 47, 100)

The Red Door Inn
1701 Water Street
Peru
815/223-2500
Reservations accepted,
   required on weekends
Credit Cards: V, MC, AE, DC, CB
(55)

Rockford Woman's Club Food Shop
2405 North Church Street
Rockford
815/968-5719
No reservations
No credit cards
(46, 95, 105)

Maldaner's
222 South Sixth Street
Springfield
217/522-4313
Reservations accepted
Credit cards: V, MC
(9, 10)

The Intermezzo Pastry Shop
Krannert Center for the Performing Arts
500 South Goodwin Avenue
Urbana
217/333-8412
No reservations
No credit cards
(14, 99, 115)

Rick's, An American Cafe
Sunnycrest Mall #15,
1717 South Philo Road
Urbana
217/384-8111
Reservations recommended
Credit cards:
(71, 82, 83, 88, 96, 103, 114)

Le Francais
269 South Milwaukee Street
Wheeling
312/541-7470
Reservations mandatory
Credit cards: V, MC, AE, DC
(29, 52, 107)

Melange Restaurant
1515 Sheridan Street, Plaza del Lago
Wilmette
312/256-1700
Reservations suggested
Credit cards: V, MC, AE, DC
(25, 37, 72, 87)

Index